Wash It Away

Memoir of a Rape Survivor

ML Bilby

WASH IT AWAY

Published 2016 by Quinn's Bookshelf

Library of Congress Cataloging-in-Publication Data

Bilby, Mary
Wash It Away / ML Bilby

First Printing May 2016

10 9 8 7 6 5 4 3 2 1

DEDICATION

To all the brave women who have survived the trauma of rape, may they find peace. And to our family and friends, may they have a better understanding of the horror we had to endure in order to return to them. For some of us the journey may never be over, for others your journey has just begun. Raise your head high, as you take each step towards a new future, and with pride tell your story. Remember, our story does not define who we are. We are no longer victims, we are ... *SURVIVORS.*

CONTENTS

CONTENTS

ACKNOWLEDGMENTS

I would like to thank my dear friends Christine Davidson, Arlene Hawkins and Shirley Kirk Pickle for their shoulders to lean on and encouragement during the writing of this book.

Arlene was the first person to read the draft of my book. It was her words of encouragement and non-judgmental attitude that helped drive me to focus on finalizing my story for publication.

As I began to trust in my friends, and let my story flow through their ears, it was Christine who spoke to me with an open heart, which allowed me to trust that my story had value to others. It was her questions that encouraged me to reveal more of my story than I had intended.

When asked to read my book and give her comments, without hesitation Shirley was there for me. She read and re-read, her insight helped my story to open wider. This is when I knew it was time to share my story with you, the reader.

Ladies, you have helped turn this into a wonderful experience.

Thank You!

Wash It Away

Memoir of a Rape Survivor

Except for the friends and family who have given
permission to appear in this book, all names and all
identifying characteristics of individuals mentioned
have been changed in order to protect their privacy.

The Surf Was Singing to Me

The day was September 14, 2004, and I had just finished my walk along the shoreline of Misquamicut Beach. As I approached the spot where I had set up my chair and all that baggage necessary for such an outing, something stopped me in my tracks. Looking out at the horizon, it was such a clear day, I could see the bluffs on Block Island or so it seemed. The sun's rays beat ever so gently on my skin, as a cool breeze brushed my face to dry away my tears. It was as if the surf was singing to me. Yes, the song was for me alone. "You are free ... you have set yourself free!" As I listened to the chant of the sea, the surf pounding into shore and dredging back into the deep all the impurities of this sand beneath my feet, I felt cleansed. Deep inside I could feel God's love; He was inside my being, protecting me. Oh Lord, thank you for this day.

There was a time, not so long ago that I was caught in the rip tide of life and as hard as I tried I could not swim back to shore. This forty-seven-year-old, one-hundred-thirty-five-pound, Italian grandmother of two, feared she was going to die. The mind is so powerful. Like Pandora's box all locked up in this deep black hole on Memory Island, never to allow the demons to escape ... I was safe, memories erased, life was wonderful.

Is anyone interested? Does anyone care? It's not just my story – it's the story of every Rape Survivor. And YES, I am a "Survivor" and this is my story.

Everyone has difficult times in his or her life and sometimes you need to seek counseling from a professional. There you have it, the year is 2000 and Mary is in counseling, coming to terms with the past, divorce, father's death and problems at work.

Just life, just the normal everyday issues. But, now my health is declining and Doctor Brown, who has been my doctor for most of my adult life, is getting concerned and has ordered a series of tests just to rule out, whatever. Doctor Brown never cracks a smile, but under that white beard, which compensates for his balding head, I can see the corners of his lips curl up just a bit with approval as I say, "I'm not really concerned, but oh well, I do have insurance so let's go for it."

It's not often I'm at the hospital, hope I don't run into anyone I know. You know how gossip flies and they'll have you on your deathbed when it's just a cold. Quickly my feet take me to the check-in counter where I am instructed to continue down the hall to a separate waiting room for patients having similar testing. As I walk into this room, my eyes are scanning for the availability of a seat. Across the room an empty chair rests against the sterile gray walls and I quickly claim refuge in its cushion. It was like musical chairs; as patients left, seats were taken by the on-flowing traffic of new arrivals. Some were young, and there were the old, the friends, the happy and the sad. As I looked around the room, I couldn't help but wonder what their stories were and what cards had life dealt them. For me, I was content, had made it through a divorce after twenty-five years of marriage. My parents had taken me in, which had helped to alleviate my financial burden. My three grown sons were healthy; they too had escaped our divorce fairly unscathed and had moved on with their lives.

All this chatter.... the TV, you can't get away from it. Even in the waiting room it has to be blaring. Too lazy to get up and walk across the room to get a magazine, I too, sat there like most, staring at that TV. My body felt strange and my heart started to beat rapidly out of control and my whole being was shaking. Why? Those words spoken sent a fear throughout me. Why? It's just a program about Post-Traumatic Stress Disorder (PTSD). They are talking about men and the trauma of war, but as the conversation unfolds, the word *RAPE* is spoken, and my uncontrolled reaction was scaring me and I didn't know why.

Then my name was called; it was my turn to walk down that cold, silent corridor for testing. At that exact moment, a toll-free phone number was flashing across the screen and the announcer was saying these words, "If you or someone you know is suffering from post-traumatic stress there is help." What possessed me to hurriedly jot the number down? Something is wrong, what is it? What am I thinking? After all the formalities of the x-rays and blood work were done, I walked out to the parking lot and to my car with only one thought. I have a secret but I don't know what it is.

By the time I had approached my parents' home, my home, the anxiety in my mind had reached such a point that walking through the front door was overwhelming. Oh, Lord, just get me to the sofa. Who is that child sitting Indian style, rocking, crying, possessed by what? The harder I cried the faster I rocked. Mary, stop! You must get control. I talk to myself all the time, sometimes I even take my own advice and this was one of those times.

Where is that damned number? Do you know how many pieces of paper one can collect at the bottom of one's purse? Swiftly I turned my purse upside down and began shaking it with the rage of an insane woman. Stuff was flying everywhere – if only I could empty my head as quickly. I found it, the number. My heart was pounding as I dialed the number. Oh, what will I say to the person on the other end? The phone stopped ringing and it's just a recorded message. "Leave your name and address and information will be sent to you." CLICK ... the phone hung up, I hung up! Leave my name and address, am I crazy? I can't do this – okay, Mary, get strong, what is there to be afraid of? It's just a recording. Pick up the damned phone, dial the bloody number, and leave your damned address. "Oh, God, help me," I cried. My hands were shaking and it felt as though I was watching myself through the eyes of someone else as I dialed the number again. My heart rate slowed down as the phone stopped ringing and this time the recorded message was less threatening to my ears. With a crackling voice I proceed to give both my name and address, then CLICK ... it's over. I did it.

As I lean back into the sofa with legs curled up into my chest, my lips touch the flesh of my knees and instinctively my arms caress my legs. The sounds echo from the walls of this old house as my lips repetitively give love to this flesh. What is that scent? Do I smell the cologne embedded in the fiber of the fabric of my father's favorite chair? The chair that my mother will not move from its spot - the chair my father was sitting in when he died that dreadful June morning in 1999.

The morning started out so happy and full of excitement for the upcoming trip to California. This was to be a family reunion of my mother's siblings; my Mother was not as excited as my Father. He was always up for an adventure. I remember a time when they were invited to go to France with friends, and Mother said "No!" She just dug her heels in and would not go. They missed out on a wonderful trip and memories were not created. This time my father was not taking "No!" He agreed with her siblings and felt that, as they all were getting on in age, this reunion must take place before one of them was to meet their demise. My mother didn't want to go, she said she just had this strange feeling that something wasn't right. My father and I just brushed it off as Mom just hesitating about getting into that big bird and flying away. We should have known better. Mom always had these strange feelings, like the time she thought something was wrong in her throat and the doctor said everything was okay. Mom persisted and eventually her doctor gave in and did more testing – Mom was right, she had thyroid cancer, encapsulated on one side. She had the surgery and we all were glad afterward that she was so insistent about her intuition.

The morning of the trip Mom and I were sitting in the living room. Their suitcases were all packed and waiting by the front door for my brother to arrive and transport them to the airport in Providence for their flight. The weather was perfect, blue skies, a touch of a breeze in the air and not a cloud to be found. The scent of late blooming lilacs penetrated each breath we inhaled as this light breeze found its way through the windows. Oh what a calming effect the fragrance had on us as we spoke of the great time she would have and I remember her comment about taking pictures to bring back home.

We could hear the lawnmower from what we thought was the neighbor next door. "It's not the neighbor, it's your dad mowing the grass; what the hell is he doing?" Mom yells as she walks to the sun-room. She yells out at him and his reply was, "I just want to make sure everything is done before we leave, go back in the house, Mary" (my mom's name is Mary, too). Her reply was, "Okay, Gene, suit yourself – but mowing the grass in your suit?" We no sooner had walked across the orange shag carpet into the paneled living room when my Father ran in behind us yelling, "Something's wrong ... something's wrong."

He headed straight for his recliner and attempted to recline it, my Mother ran to the kitchen sink to get a glass of water, I heard the water running but it's too late. I stood over my Father and as I looked down, I realized, "Something is wrong and maybe this was what my Mother was sensing all along." There was a cold chill going down my back as I watched his limbs begin to stiffen out straight and his whole body shook as if he was possessed by a demon. The chair even moved a bit. He looked so clammy as sweat rolled across his face. Oh, no ... "Mom stay back, call 911 ... call 911!" She ran to the phone and all I could think was stay calm, stay calm. By now his dark brown eyes were rolling back, those dark brown eyes, I'll never see them again.

I immediately grabbed my Father's arm and tried to take his pulse ... no, where is it, where is it? Tears erupted and my voice quivered as Mom handed me the phone and the voice on the other end started throwing questions at me and all I could hear is Mom crying in the background. "It's my father, I think he just had a heart attack and I can't get a pulse." "What's your address?" the voice asked. "It's 26 Nutmeg Drive." "Okay, just stay calm, help is on the way, clear the entrance so they can get the stretcher in." It was as if we were in a time-warp, it was such a joyful day, how could we be here like this?

So, no, it's not the scent of cologne embedded in the fiber of the fabric of my father's favorite chair. It's the scent of fear. Fear escaping from every pore of this aging flesh. And fear that is embedded in the fiber of this sofa, the sofa where my Mother sits and mourns for life past.

Two months have passed and I am unable to escape the counseling sessions, it would be deadly for me to try. Did you know panic attacks could prevent you from focusing? Fear causes your heart to race ever so fast, which causes your breathing to become rapid. This vicious cycle drains the spirit and hypnotizes the mind and you are alone in this world you have created. One moment feeling protected, guarded, and the next, vulnerable and in danger. I want to be at peace and Doctor Brown said that Paxil would help – he thinks I'm just depressed, after all I'm a woman, the weaker sex, and everyone gets depressed these days. That's the answer for everything, pop that little pink pill!

Ms. Zest, my counselor, has another take on things, and up to this point the focus of our sessions has been on my childhood, our dysfunctional family and the constant badgering and abusive treatment I had been subjected to at work. There was no room or time allotted for other issues. Up to this point I didn't know there were other issues. To make progress in therapy it's important to trust and feel comfortable with your counselor. Trust me, I know ever so well; I went through many counselors during my divorce years - men, women, young, seasoned, those recommended and those just chosen from the yellow pages of the local phone book. But, Ms. Zest, this slightly overweight lady, was quite the find. First I thought, a little strange, not the typical sessions. Me sitting in a rocking chair trying to unburden myself, as she just sits at her desk with one leg curled under her derrière, the other leg dangling, and ever so often she would glance over the top rim of her glasses as she munches away on her dinner. I can't help but scan the room to notice a large bookcase with many shelves and children's toys piled high on each. Then, another bookcase with adult self-help books and beside my chair is a table holding only a tissue box.

The walls are painted in this muted gray color. This is a color that buffers emotions and never gives way to life's song; this is the birthing room of secrets and the burial ground of pain. The painter of this room must have been in prison or so it would appear, for only a prisoner would welcome such bleakness. In the distance I hear a faint sound and remember the train station is not that far away; the comforting sounds of the train whistle could be heard through the pane windows of this second-floor room.

Was she listening? Did she really hear what I was saying? At least we made eye contact so I think she must be listening or, maybe not. Just when I think NOT, Ms. Zest would toss back her dark brown hair and give me that look, and I just know here it comes. "Mary," she says in that high-pitched voice of hers, "And you haven't spoken of Paul, what's going on there?" Paul was my first love. Yes, my husband I loved but was *never* in love with. With Paul I knew how it felt to truly love someone with every atom of one's being. My body was in a constant explosion when he was near, as was our relationship.

I had become an addict, it was an addiction that blinded me and I could not see or hear or maybe I just hoped that she, the other woman, would go away - or was *I* the other woman?

Did you ever bite into that very red polished apple, and the juice ran down the side of your mouth with each bite? So crisp, sweet, and with each bite your mouth waters as your palate screams for more. Then as you move in for that next bite a most distasteful sight, a worm. This worm, all cozy, just slithering out of that very spot you were about to place your mouth on. What has it done to that succulent juice? But it

16

tasted so good, what do you do, throw it away? Eat around it? How can you truly enjoy the pleasures of your senses once spoil sets in? I tell Ms. Zest all, and another session is down. She looks at the clock and that's my cue to wipe away those salty tears. We set the next appointment and say our good-byes with arms wrapped around each other. Sometimes the best part of our sessions is the hugs, as just a caress can have so much healing power.

A few days have passed and I'm sitting on the sofa at home reading, when out of the corner of my eye there is a shadow blocking the light. It's the mail truck and like the visual icon on my computer and those neon lights in the window of the local liquor store, which cannot be ignored, I respond. Out the door I go, heading down the driveway and straight for that box on a stick. As I pulled the door of the mailbox open, I found a brown wrapped package among the mail. I knew by the address on the outside that this was the information that recorded message had promised would come. I was anxious to get the package open and find out if this little package would hold the key to Pandora's box.

Once inside the house I sat down in the middle of the living room on the floor and tore open the package to find a video cassette "Life After Trauma – What Every Person Should Know." My hands started to shake and all the emotions first felt at the hospital, those fears and scary thoughts, just bits and pieces, started flashing in my mind. Something BAD happened to me. I hesitantly slipped the cassette in to play and after a few minutes turned it off. Why was it hard to watch?

Post-Traumatic Stress Disorder (PTSD) affects one in thirteen Americans and can occur after exposure to an extreme traumatic event such as sudden unexpected death. Okay, that's one – my brother was killed in a car accident at age thirty-one and my father died at age sixty-nine of a sudden heart attack, right before my eyes. That's life, it's under control, I dealt with it, "So, calm down, Mary," talking to myself again. "Turn the video cassette back on and stop shaking, it's just information."

Like a volcano erupting, tears rolled down my face. It was difficult for me to listen to the video but I forced myself to finish watching and hearing the words, *physical and sexual assaults*. These words sent painful emotions throughout me. Well, as confused as I felt about my reactions, I had completed the video then sat on the sofa rocking back and forth and crying, knowing that I had been assaulted. My spirit was telling me so and you must believe your spirit. The only thing I remember was fear and pain.

Days passed and a couple of weeks went by, then one evening in my session with Ms. Zest this all came out and we explored my childhood again. As with most families mine was no exception, we had our share of dysfunctional periods and that too had passed. This exploration did serve to help me slay many a demon, all but the one I was searching for. If I wasn't crazy when these sessions started, I was beginning to question the wellness of my mind now. Any sane person would not want to live in the chambers of this mind, as only the sick and feeble could survive here. To be afraid of every man in view, not just strangers but even your sons and hoping to hide the fear behind a mask of comedy. Over these past weeks I've used my share of tissues to wipe my tears. This session is over and it's time to put the mask back on and step out into the world again.

The Baseball Cap

If you are a mother, then you can identify with the overwhelming joy I felt each time the doorbell rang, and this most handsome young man would be standing outside the door calling on me. Each time he called, the feelings and thoughts were always the same. As I approached the door the first sight through the small overhead windows of the front door, was of this wonderful baseball cap and I knew my only late night, unannounced callers were either my youngest son Chris, or Paul. I was always so full of joy at the sight of either of them, that sometimes it felt as if I were walking on air as I was approaching the door. But, today in 2001…that baseball cap sent shock waves of fear through every nerve in my body.

My hands were trembling as I clenched the doorknob, slowly turned this icy cold metal and pulled the door open; who would be on the other side of this door? Then with relief I felt a calmness come over me as if someone had just wrapped his loving arms around me and then I heard, "Hi, Mom." The love of one's son can wash away *almost* anything. Big hugs from this six-foot-tall adorable man who comes calling at all hours, especially if he needs to talk. Once he was inside, the door was locked and bolted like a fortress. The boys always joked about Mom locking them in. They'd say, "Mom, why do you lock the door, it's daytime? Who's going to get you? The kids will be going in and out, why lock the door?" Well, Mary, what chamber of your mind were you just traveling? Where did this fear come from?

Like a puppy following his master, I followed my son through the living room and into the kitchen. There sat Chris at the kitchen snack bar ... my baby, twenty-six-years-old and all grown up. As we visited I couldn't help but wonder if he could sense the love that is his. Our conversation shifts from, "How are you doing, Mom?" to, "I need your opinion." Many of our conversations started and ended this way and the fact that he values what I have to say struck emotions in my heart that said to me – I have value!

The hardest thing for a mother is to let go and see your children as adults. At the end of the evening we said our good-byes and as he held me in his arms, I kissed his cheek and in doing so, my face was pricked by his dark brown mustache. Not wanting to let go but realizing it was time - we walked to the door, then Chris turned, smiled and the words, "I love you" rolled from our lips. As he walked through the doorway, across the yard and to his car, that same heart that just felt so much joy was experiencing emptiness. With this, a deep breath of the crisp cool night air is inhaled, exhaled, and I let go of that emptiness and closed the door.

Have you heard the saying, "Don't get too comfortable in your skin"?" Well, don't! It was late, maybe close to midnight when Chris left, and I was tired and could not wait to lay my head down. So up the carpeted stairs I started, but midway that fear surged again and deja vu ... memories were erupting from within and the vision of someone being battered on those very stairs was so vivid. Who was she? Was it memories of my father beating my mother?   Was it flashbacks from a movie? My legs, with a mind of their own, began running fast up the stairs to my room as if someone were chasing me. My imagination, I thought, it's just images in my mind. Quickly I changed into my pajamas and climbed into bed, then proceeded to speak to the Lord.

"Lord, please help me! What does all this mean and what do You want me to see?" Trying to relax with tearful eyes closed ever so tightly and trying to rid myself of this 'fight or flight' reaction, I thought if I could only lock out these images maybe sleep would take over. I do not remember falling asleep but the vision of sunlight shining through the prism in the bedroom window and casting rainbows on every wall was quite breath-taking. Have you ever woken in the middle of a rainbow? It's the most beautiful sight as various shades of color dance about with gaiety. The heavens are saying, "Good Morning" and you can't help but smile and a new day begins.

Days and weeks passed and a multitude of images unfolded. It's amazing how just a certain word, phrase, fragrance or motion can unleash memories that were buried so deep in the chambers of one's mind. The key to Pandora's box has been found and the horror and the memory of the rape have been released into my consciousness ... it is alive.

My parents had traveled for twenty years, spending winters in Florida so not much time or money was spent on updating or repairs to their home, a Cape Cod style, modest home built in the early 1960's with dark paneled walls and dark orange shag carpeting in every room on the first floor. When I moved in during my divorce the second floor became my sanctuary, so after much hard work, two coats of primer and paint (off white in color) covered the forest green walls.

With a Victorian flare, the second floor had been transformed and even my mother would climb the stairs to escape the gloom of the dark cloud below.

After my father died I tried to convince my mother to paint over the dark paneled walls of the first floor. "Let's cheer this place up," I said, but she wouldn't hear of changing anything my father had done, and the cloud of gloom remains.

My mother, now seventy-one, has just traveled to Florida to pack up all belongings and bring them home to Rhode Island. This will be her last trip, for without her husband to vacation with, the desire to travel does not exist. Luckily for me, she is in Florida and I am alone, I am free. Yes, I just want to be free ... free from the past, free from the unknown and free to move forward with my life.

Now it's time to test the waters and with the dosage of Paxil increased, both Doctor Brown and Ms. Zest approve of my return to the workforce. Am I ready? The reason I was out was due to the images, flashbacks of the unknown. Afraid of failure I decided to increase the dosage just a bit more and like a child leaving for the first day of school, off I went and was ready to meet any challenge that came my way. There was nothing going to rattle me on this first day. By now the twelve weeks of FMLA (family medical leave act) had expired. Things at work had not changed, but I had changed and with therapy and medication could now control my reactions to all the demands. Just as the birth control pill helps with unwanted pregnancies, this little pink pill (Paxil) sheltered me from unwanted stress. It appeared that my life was back on track and I loved being back at work with my friends. And within weeks even my social life was increasing and I had a sense of normalcy again - a plateau had been reached and I was sailing through time with joy.

At home one weekend, walking down the stairs in my stocking feet to the first floor, carrying a laundry basket, I slipped on the stairs. Holding the basket tight, afraid it was going to fly out of my hands and slam into the mirrored table at the bottom of the stairs, I fell against the wall then down the stairs, never leaving hold of the basket and when I hit the floor, "Thank the Lord." That's all I could think. Thank God, the table with mirror attached did not get damaged. Then I began shouting out loud, "Oh! ... Oh, my God! That's what happened. Someone attacked me on the stairs, I remember!"

I started to cry and yell out loud, "This can't be, no, this can't be." My head was hurting; it felt like it had been struck with a baseball bat. There were images of me being thrown against the wall and I could remember the pain I felt in my head. Then seeing myself being forced against the stairs and fighting to get away, then falling into the mirrored table. By now my legs were shaking and I ran to the sofa, sat there crying, rocking and staring at that table with fear and anger. Was I not as important as that table? As my eyes shifted from the table to the floor in front of the door, more memories started to flood out and there I was, lying on the floor, head pressed against the base of that table, eyes staring up at the front door ahead. I can't remember anything else.

Who was there, how badly was I hurt? As real as it seemed and as painful as it all felt there was still this question. Was this really and truly a memory, did this happen? This is something you read about or see in a movie. I was trying not to panic, and the only person I could talk to would be Ms. Zest. Where is her number? She had given me her home number in case of an emergency; she said, "Call at any time," because I had been having thoughts of suicide. In fact, there was one attempt already during my divorce. As I drove in the dark of night down this country road, feeling desperate and unloved, I locked into the sight of the headlights coming towards me, a semi-truck. In a daze, as the headlights drew me in, I raced across my lane into the oncoming lights. I remember thinking, "I want it over, I just want to end my life."

All of a sudden, my daze was broken by the sound of the blaring horn from the semi-truck and I quickly turned the wheel and bolted across the lane and landed off the side of the road. It must not have been my time to leave this earth and luckily for me we were the only vehicles on this country road. Time stood still as I gripped the steering wheel, just staring into the night. Now I'm shaking and my heart is pounding so hard that my chest hurts, and as I quiver in the night all I could think was that I almost killed myself, what was I thinking? How could I do this to my sons? If I knew anything, I knew that ... they were my reason to live.

My legs did not want to move but after some effort I was up and off to find her number and that meant the walk across the floor, past the front door, past the mirrored table and up the stairs. This horrible dirty feeling came over me. I suddenly felt ashamed. Once up the stairs and in my living room the routine of dumping out my purse to find her number began. With the number found, I called Ms. Zest and left a message. And don't you know the one time I called her at home and where was she? "Ms. Zest, please call me, I need you!" My voice was cracking so much I hoped she could understand the message. All I could do now was wait for her call. To pass the time and try to calm down, I turned on the television and after a time was able to focus a bit.

It was getting late and there was work in the morning, "She must be out for the evening," I thought. Well, I'll call her from work in the morning, this was my plan. As my footsteps approached the bedroom the phone rang. "Oh, please let it be

Ms. Zest." By now it was near midnight and yes, it was she. "Mary, are you okay?" she asked, and my response was "Yes, I've calmed down." We talked briefly about the evening events and set an appointment for Monday evening. I had such a feeling of relief after our conversation and I knew she couldn't make this all go away but talking it out with her always eases my anxiety and opens up more of the truth. What was the truth? What was the significance of that table? It's just a piece of furniture, a dead hunk of carved wood.

Off to bed, I closed my eyes and buried my face into my pillow to soak up the fresh fragrance of the fabric softener, and after a while I must have fallen asleep. My eyes were starting to open but I was so warm, all curled up in the fetal position, and as my eyes opened fully, I could feel warm, almost hot water hitting my body. It stung like many needles penetrating my skin. As I went to uncurl myself and stand up I found that I was not in bed, but in the bathtub. How did I get here? I don't remember anything. My body was so red, I could have scalded myself - but I had felt so safe and comfortable before I opened my eyes.

Standing in the tub reaching for the knob to turn off the shower, it was as if I were a robot, with no emotions. I pulled the curtain back and stepped with one foot and then the other over the side of the tub. Then reaching for my blue towel, which was draped across the toilet seat, I dried myself off and attempted to proceed with my morning routine of dressing for work. But I found myself standing and staring into the bedroom closet; my mind was shut down and turned off. This robot must be reprogrammed or she'll never get off to work. This wasn't the first time I had mysteriously found myself climbing out of the tub in the morning. Okay, I can do this!

Now the challenging part, to walk down those stairs, past the table and through the front door. With each step there were flashbacks of that night, fighting, the pain ... that awful pain, more pieces to complete the memory. Well, I made it through that door and without an intrusion (no demons attacked me) and into my car and off to work, knowing that I would see Ms. Zest at 6:00 P.M. that evening. What will the outcome be? Already I missed that water. Why?!?

Maybe I shouldn't have gone to work and looking back I know it was not a safe thing to do – I had taken an extra dose of Paxil that morning and could barely function at work. I was virtually non-productive and spent most of the time staring at the walls in my small cubicle or computer monitor. Was this the reason my responses were not quick? Since returning to work I've noticed the lack of concentration and difficulty in remembering just ... the very little things. Post-it-notes were everywhere in an attempt to stay on top of things. What a mistake I made, maybe no one will notice, after all I'm not important.

The Employee Relations staff is located near my cubicle and it's not unusual to hear very emotional employees crying as they plead their cases. The noise level in the surrounding areas are always loud either with excitement of conversations or just the sounds of shuffling feet of employees, as they pass by and visit from cube to cube, and I can hear faint sounds of music through the walls that enclose my cubicle. Ever so often I'd glance up at the employees as they paraded by and wonder if anyone recognized this mask that I wore. I'm only one of ten thousand employees, how can it be that I am the privileged one? Where is my soul mate? There must be someone who sees his reflection in my face. The difference in my behavior has not been noticed and that being said, the workday is over and I'm off to meet Ms. Zest for our session.

Walking out the casino door in single file, we stand, waiting, then one by one we step into the bus and find our seat. Like cattle herded into a wagon being sent to the butcher, we pile in, standing in the aisle way, bodies pressed against each other. I was not going to be crowded in like cattle, so when I stepped into the bus I stood next to the driver's seat and waved everyone by. "Go ahead, I'm not moving from this spot, pass by, keep moving." Stumbling over my words at times, but the job was done and as the driver closed the door, I stepped in front of the aisle; *claustrophobia* was now behind me, as was a young Asian girl. My arms were wrapped loosely around the metal pole just to help steady my stance. My eyes were focused through the pane of glass ahead as nature's cleansing rain exploded onto the windshield then disappeared repeatedly as the black straight arm of destruction, like a pendulum, slapped back and forth … bang, bang. I had pleasant thoughts of a child running and splashing in puddles then standing straight and tall, imitating a Goddess. She raises her hands to the heavens and with mouth open wide and tongue stretched out as to catch the raindrops and drink this holy water falling from the sky. I love the rain today, as I did as a child.

As the bus approaches the employee parking garage this childhood memory fades; like cattle we have arrived safely and herd out with speed to the elevators and our escape home. The effects of the Paxil have weakened from the morning hours, my words are spoken with confidence and my sensors are on high alert. Then my escape into the elevator in the mix of genders and again we are crowded, door closes and I am trapped against the back wall in this stench of smoke and perspiration. Too late I've just inhaled – now I must hold my breath until the door opens. Do I close my eyes? Do I stare into the camera? I am claustrophobic and must talk myself into composure. Staring above the sea of heads, the crack where the two metal doors meet opens and again the cattle flee.

As I stepped out onto the garage floor, a cool breeze kissed my face and I exhaled the old and inhaled the new fresh, cool, stimulating air, lungs expanded to full capacity and holding for a few seconds before exhaling. "Composure, Mary." Words spoken to myself. This routine walk through the garage to my car was memorized. First, I must locate the cameras to make sure my every step is in view. Second, scan the surrounding areas, noticing who is standing where and with whom. Once my internal surveillance was in check, the walk through the garage toward my car began. My eyes were scanning empty spaces between parked cars, noticing movements of any kind. My heart was racing in anticipation of the unknown. Never, never walking to one side or the other but straight in the path of any car driving through the garage. It would be easier to dodge an oncoming car than to escape the arms of an attacker. There were nights this walk was less stressed, shared with friends, but not this night and every sound shouted the false alarm of danger.

It was about a forty-five minute drive in the pouring rain from work in Connecticut to her office in Westerly, just enough time to engage the mind and body in a boxing match, or was it a debate on where the greater damage was. The mind is screaming, "You are dirty and shameful and need to be cleansed," and my body is crying out in pain of the flesh. I kept thinking "If only I could peel off my skin and cut away my vaginal area, it would be over and I would be rid of this nightmare."The vision of him on me, that thrusting motion; caused this instant reflex in the pit of my stomach and I could smell the stench erupting from my mouth.

With the boxing match over, I had arrived safely in town. Then I parked the car and ran splashing through the puddles to the office door. This impulse to cut this private part of my body away is getting stronger. It was no longer private. I hate! Yes, hate that painful vile piece of flesh. "Now Mary, clear your head, open the door and get on with your session." Thinking out loud and talking to myself again. As I walked through the door, Ms. Zest greets me with a huge hug. I must say, a most welcomed hug, and I just held on to soak in all the energy she could share. As always when I looked into her chocolate brown eyes, I could feel reassured that whatever is haunting me she will help me to draw it out. As good a listener as she is, Ms. Zest is capable of dosing out the wickedest of tongue lashings that one could expect to receive and this was that moment ... here it comes! About halfway through the session we had covered last night in detail and my reactions were calmer, she lit into me about abusing the medication and I promised that I would only take the prescribed dosage in the future.

Then she turned back to the night's events and me being in the bathtub in the water. She described this as a cleansing, a way for the mind to wash away the events and that it also could represent the safest place, going back to the mother's womb, surrounded by water. This is a very safe and pure time in one's life and there is nothing that can harm you.

We discussed this fearful table and what would have transpired if the table had broken. As a child growing up in the 1950's, I knew punishment always followed an accident where material objects got broken. All my friends received the same sort of punishment – if you knocked over your glass of milk, you were wasteful and deserved a smack on the hand. But if the glass broke, it was a good old-fashioned paddling on the backside. Then in the 1960's, as a teen, the paddling turned to strapping with a leather belt and if you were lucky, the buckle would miss your flesh. Those were the times and approved punishment, unlike today. By today's standards that would be classified as abusive punishment, not tolerated. Nonetheless, children of the 50's grew up to be healthy and respectful adults, but maybe a little scared. I loved my father but the fear of upsetting or not pleasing him remained all my adult life. All little girls want to be seen as good little girls in their dad's eyes. Was that it, I was afraid the table was going to be damaged, even broken, during the fight? Ms. Zest agreed this was one of the underlying fears.

When the session was over, she made me promise there would be NO cutting of the body and I would call her or a friend immediately if the impulse could not be controlled. Then, she gave me her cell phone number and said, "I know you won't take advantage of my privacy and will only use this number in an emergency." In just a few months she has gotten to know the Mary that no one knows or will ever really know. Reaching for a tissue, I dry my eyes then freshen up my makeup while Ms. Zest checks her calendar for the next available date, and the appointment is set for two weeks. She will be out of town and keeping this in mind, she jots down her associate's phone number, just to cover all bases, and then she can enjoy her trip, knowing I'll be covered. We say our good-byes.

One of Ms. Zest's goals was to counsel me to a point that the word rape or sexual assault would replace the softer word "incident." That's how I'd refer to the rape. No incident occurred that night! This was not an accident but a premeditated act of violence. He forced himself on me - I was not! Never! Never was I willing. Trying to say this word repulses me, my face becomes twisted, my shoulders roll upward and the impulse generated in my torso to curl forward takes hold as my face falls downward with shame. Why do I still blame myself? Why can't I forgive myself?

The Onlooker

One's life goes on, day after day the usual routines. You go to work, meet with friends, entertain guests at home and all appears normal to the Onlooker. Yes, have you ever gone to an art show? If so, than you were the Onlooker, standing ever so intently staring at the one piece that captured your attention. Can you see past the painted canvas? Can you feel the intense emotions that guided the artist's every stroke? But, don't feel slighted to be referred to as the Onlooker, as we are all artists, too, painting our life story with many shades and techniques. The Lord has laid out a very pure canvas on which our brush may stroke freely. It is our choice, the soft calmness of watercolors or the sometimes bleakness or stormy shades of oils. Most of us transition from oils to watercolors throughout our life span, entertaining all the possibilities. What would life be without color, without choices?

So too, life passes with the stroke of my brush across the canvas. Weeks of more sessions with Ms. Zest, and this virgin canvas … is no more. I am having dreams of a man leaning over me as I lie in bed sleeping and when my eyes open, there he is staring at me, his face so close I can feel the aura of his body. Then screaming, I wake to find myself sitting upright in bed and very much alone in an empty room.

My heart is racing and it was all so real, even the screams, and over time the intensity of the dreams has grown stronger.

Then another thing to consider, the reality of all the bruises on my body. I awaken with scratches all over my back … they look like demon claws have attacked me. What about all the black and blue? I go to bed not bruised and wake up as if I have been in a fight. Sleep is a valuable commodity and one that I no longer share in. How can I? Would you be able to sleep again if upon rising you found your face all bruised and you remember nothing?

Well, mother has arrived home from her last Florida trip with a new hairdo – she has decided not to dye her hair anymore and to allow the silvery gray color to grow out. The flight was a bit delayed and it was almost midnight when she walked through the passageway. I was so glad to see her smiling face and those crystal deep-blue eyes that shimmered when the light hit them just right and I couldn't wait to wrap my arms around her. Remember that power of hugs and kisses, the touch of another human that translates to your senses that everything is safe now? I had just stepped back to my childhood for a few moments. Oh, the joys of being a child when life was uncomplicated. As the embrace releases and our eyes meet, I am here and now, the caretaker of my mother. Off to the baggage claims, to the car, down Route 95 south from T. F. Green Airport in Providence to the back roads of Westerly and home, talking non-stop. Yes, it felt good to have her back home again.

It's now summer and time to engage in my favorite sport, golf. The summer league has started and it's off to Lindbrook Country Club every Friday night to play. This is a couples' league and I used to be a couple but now I'm a single with a seventy-year-old widower for a partner, a very nice man who critiques every stroke I swing. "Patience, Mary," I say to myself ... "the season is short so just enjoy the fresh air."

It was late in the golfing season and I was standing at the second hole, looking across the fairway, and whom do I see but Paul (my love) and a male friend walking with golf bags in hand. I turned away as I didn't want him to notice me and I didn't want our eyes to exchange any glances. It's been months since we've seen or spoken to one another and best not to start up a relationship of any kind now. I loved that man so much and it's hard not to stare in his direction. Memories took me back to when we were dating and Paul often would turn to me and say "Mary, you are staring at me again." It was as if I couldn't get enough of him and I just loved the movement of his body, the facial expressions he'd make, he was so dramatic.

I remember when we first met, he had come to work at this printing company I worked at. At the time, I was just experiencing the last stages of my divorce, all that nasty stuff that goes on between a husband and wife when their marriage comes to an end. On Friday nights co-workers would get together for drinks to end the workweek on a high note. More often than not I would opt out, and just go home. Paul, noticing my uneasiness to congregate after work would insist on only the two of us meeting for coffee at a place which was closer to my home. He would not accept a "no" so we met.

And it wasn't long before the relationship began. He was quite the distraction for me and soon our time together included his weekly pool league. Then, once the budding of flowers from beneath the ground started, so did the spring golf league and Paul became my partner and we played on this very same golf course. But that was then and this is now.

Nine holes of golf played, then into the clubhouse to congregate with friends and have a late-night snack, then to my car where I found a cassette (CD) was left on the front window. Of course, I knew who had left it. It could only be Paul. 'Thunderstorm' was the title, beautiful piano music with the sounds of nature. He had seen me on the golf course and I knew now there would be future contacts. On the drive home all I could think of was Paul and his touch and how I longed to be with him. We all have expectations of how our life should turn out and mine was a forever after, Cinderella fairy tale with Paul slipping that glass shoe on my foot, and saying "I love you." My six-foot-tall, blonde-haired, blue-eyed southern Prince would carry me away. Well, those were expectations I would never see.

Not much time had passed before the phone calls started. I would screen all calls and never answer the phone again for if I did, and it was Paul, then I would be forced to remember the story of the worm in the apple, the one he chose over me. Yes, Paul and this other woman shared a life together. The past relationship with Paul drove me crazy and tore my heart apart; I was always trying to conquer his love. After his many attempts to contact me failed, Paul phoned my mother and of course, she marched up those stairs phone in hand.

Mother, not knowing the hidden secrets, not that she would care, as she was very taken by Paul, too; she only knew of our relationship as being uncomplicated and faithful. She could not understand why I would not speak with him. "Just hear him out," she said. At the bottom of the stairs mother was yelling, "Mary, get the phone" and I yelled back "No, I don't want to speak with him." Of course she knows best, up the stairs and through the doorway into my living room mother trotted, approaching me with this wide grin of sheer pleasure on her face, and she handed me the phone.

"Paul," I said, "Why are you calling me? What do you

want?" He was so concerned that I had forgotten him. He kept asking, "Did you forget me? Did you forget me?" I insisted that the matter was not up for discussion and I was not going to answer any questions. Then I asked Paul if SHE was still in his life and he assured me that she was gone and he wanted me back in his life. After a long discussion and with doubt of the sincerity of Paul's intentions, I did agree to have dinner that evening at his home.

On the drive from my home to Paul's the anxiety was building at the thought of seeing him - will I stay calm? Was this true? Is she finally gone and he is all mine? As I pulled into his driveway I began to question myself; maybe this was a mistake. Maybe, I should have stayed away. Well, too late. I quickly got out of the car before changing my mind, walked to the front door and with a very shaky right hand, pressed the doorbell. My heart was beating so loudly from my chest that the sound overshadowed the ringing of the doorbell. Before I could catch a breath, the door opened.

There he stood, just as sexy as ever, and we embraced. Now my body remembers and reacts to his touch and to the scent of his skin. This was the answer to his question. I've not forgotten him! The evening went on with so much conversation and I noticed that my emotional guard was up, but physically I was okay, not afraid of him or his caress. The inner fear that I had been experiencing when in the company of any man was gone. Why? Because he was not just any man, he was my love.

Paul cooked on the grill; we had dinner, talked more and just held each other sitting on the sofa. As the night progressed Paul asked me to stay, spend the night, just the words I longed to hear. I had wanted so badly to lie down with him and to feel the heat of his body and to be the way we were. That wasn't the case and when the morning sun rose in the sky, a new day had begun and with this new day came new discoveries. Paul had discovered in those few hours that he loved me, but was not in love with me and as he spoke those words, with tears in his eyes, my heart stopped beating and I was frozen in time, in a bubble of denial.

"It's my fault," I thought. He is just saying this because I wasn't receptive to intimacy that night. I only wanted to be held in his arms. Paul must have been thinking that my feelings had changed and he doesn't want to be rejected by me. The fear that I was losing him took hold, my mind was racing, how could I stop those words from flowing from his mouth? Oh, God ... please help me, give me the strength and courage to open my mouth. If only he knew the torment that was brewing inside the chambers of my mind, this humiliation I was hiding. The tears I could not control rolled down my cheeks, my lips trembled, my hands were so cold, but at the same time I could feel the beads of perspiration on my skin. From the bubble of denial to the reality of now, the horror was unleashed and Paul's world would never be the same.

It was so hard for me; I was just now starting to be able to say the word *rape* out loud in my sessions with Ms. Zest. Paul listened and I watched his eyes as the words flowed like a fountain. I was so afraid he was going to look at me differently, judging, and blaming or with disgust. Then he pulled me into his arms to comfort me and kept repeating, "It wasn't your fault." I went on to explain, the doorbell rang that night and I woke up, ran down the stairs seeing that baseball cap through the windows in the front door. That cap had lightened my spirit and brought joy into my world, it meant trust and love was about to come through the doorway and I was ready to entertain this pleasure. I thought it was Chris, but hoped it was Paul, and opened the door. I blamed myself now for not going to the large bay window to look out first, just to make sure who was there.

When I pulled back the door, Tony pushed his way in. He was drunk. Tony and I go back many years. His sister and I were childhood friends. One day he overheard us talking about finding boyfriends and someday getting married. We were all of sixteen years old and worried about such things. Tony was such a cute little Irish fellow always hanging around us. That day he walked up to the kitchen table where she and I were playing cards and tugged on my arm to get my attention, then announced in a confident manner, "Don't worry, I will marry you. Will you marry me?" Those sweet green eyes staring intensely in anticipation of my answer, how could I say no? I laughed it off and said, "Yes," to this brave little eight-year-old boy.

When I was going through my divorce, Tony and I dated a few times and joked about his proposal, which I had forgotten till he reminded me. When I told him we could not see each other anymore as I was dating Paul, he became angry with me. I thought this would pass in time; I was wrong.

That night Tony pushed me out of the doorway, he was standing in the living room before I knew it. Then he grabbed me and tried to kiss me, I pushed him away and tried to make idle talk, trying to find out what he wanted and trying to persuade him to leave. "Tony you're drunk, go home! We can talk tomorrow, please go home you shouldn't be here." He was drunk and kept grabbing me, forcing himself against me and as I pushed him away, his grip on my wrist would tighten. I knew it was me he wanted. As I backed away from him, he was right in my face and I could not get away. The smell of booze was on his breath and I felt so small and weak, and I didn't realize I was backing myself so close to the wall. This six-foot-tall, two-hundred-pound man had trapped me up against the stairs and I could not reason with him. And the harder I tried to push him away, the stronger his grip on me became. My legs started to shake with fear – my whole body was trembling as my heart raced and I remember yelling; I could hear my voice stutter as I begged him to let me go.

"Think what you're doing, what would your family think of you? Tony, you have a girlfriend...go home to her. Please leave." His words: "No! Not yet...just kiss me," rang over and over in my ears. What else could be said to convince him to abandon this mission and leave? "You're hurting me, please stop!" These words meant nothing to him.

He had smacked me against the stairs, then I pulled myself up and tried to get away; again he hit me into the wall. I was horrified; my head was in such pain from the slam against the wall. We were fighting and I fell into the mirrored table at the bottom of the stairs. I knew he was going to rape me and I fought with all the power in my body, but I could not overpower him. This was beyond comprehension – this was a friend - not happening. I tried to stay strong but eventually the reality of my nightmare consumed me.

With the next blow I was lying on my back on the floor, head pressed against that table and crying, and he was on top of me, his green eyes staring as cold as ice. Where is that adorable little boy who once asked me to marry him? What happened to transform those sweet green eyes into ice and a heart just as cold? He was too strong; I begged, "Please don't do this.....please. Why, Tony?" "The sex must be good, he's only with you because the sex must be good." Those were his words.

I felt my body become stiff, stiff as a board, and I stared, finding that focal point on the door just like in my Lamaze class. Focus on that one spot and focus on a pleasant thought and you can block out the pain. All these random thoughts rushing to surface like a rescue boat, how can I be thinking of a seminar I once took? It was a video of inmates in a prison who were interviewed on why they rape and what excites them – they enjoy the fight. The speaker at this seminar had suggested that if you are not a virgin, then it could save your life if you did not fight.

Tony had pulled my pajama bottoms off, he had my hands pinned down and my body was frozen in fear. All I could see was Paul's face smiling down at me and I kept chanting, "Paul stay with me, don't leave me." Over and over the same words. "Paul, stay with me, don't leave me, hold me in your arms, hold me tight, stay with me." Chanting over and over again in my mind.

As the story unraveled, Paul held me in his arms, stroking my hair, my head buried into his chest. Choking back tears and voice quivering, I relived the horror of that night over again, exposing my shame and humiliation, the feeling of being worthless, less important than a piece of furniture -- that table. This little girl feared her father if the table was damaged, this grandmother feared the rapist for her safety, this mother feared the resentment in the eyes of her children, and Mary just feared for her life. No, the police were never notified, charges were not filed and the rapist walked away, but not out of my life.

Aftermath of Rape
by Mary

Tainted memories of the past
Haunting images of tangled flesh
Cries hurdled out in fright
Images of those sights
Painful labors bring new life

Haunting memories of those sights
Eyes fixed on my Knight
Snake's tongue whispers in my ear
Demons, Demons, everywhere

Eyes fixed on my Knight
Tangled flesh and horrid sights
Painful thoughts and frozen nights
Baby cries and mother dies

Eyes fixed on my Knight
Snake slithers in the night
Warm waters soothe my soul
Painful labors bring new life

Eyes fixed on my Knight!
Eyes fixed on my Knight!

The Pin

The significance of a safety pin is to hold something firmly together, such as a woman's blouse. Most women have at one time or another used a pin to replace that lost button and, not only does it prevent your exposure, it prevents the cold breeze from chilling your flesh.

In 1968 in debate of whether she deserved it or not – "She asked for it! Don't tell me she was telling the truth. How can she say he held her hands down, unpinned her pants, then raped her?" This man continued, "I was on the jury and we found him innocent!" These words were spoken by a man I was very close to at the time. He was so adamant that this woman had asked for it – "She got what she deserved." I just listened.

From my own experience, I can tell you no woman wants to be raped. No woman deserves to be raped. No woman asks to be raped. Thirty-plus years after hearing his remarks, if I were given the opportunity to debate this topic, my words would echo with authority. "I've been there. I know!"

The ignorance of 1968 lingers, and in spite of how far we think we've come, as a society there will always be those who feel, "She got what she deserves."

***

Did you know that sexual assault still occurs at rates that approximate those first identified more than twenty years ago? Estimates also vary regarding how likely a victim is to report victimization. Traditionally, rape notification rates differed depending on whether the victim knew the perpetrator — those who knew a perpetrator were often less likely to report the crime. One study revealed that approximately 1.9 million women are physically assaulted annually in the United States. The study used a definition of rape that includes forced vaginal, oral, and anal intercourse. The majority of rapes and sexual assaults perpetrated against women and girls in the United States between 1992 and 2000 were not reported to the police. Only 36 percent of rapes, 34 percent of attempted rapes, and 26 percent of sexual assaults were reported. Reasons for not reporting assault vary among individuals, but one study identified the following as common:

1. Self-blame or guilt.

2. Shame, embarrassment, or desire to keep the assault a private matter.

3. Humiliation or fear of the perpetrator or other individual's perceptions.

4. Fear of not being believed or of being accused of playing a role in the crime.

5. Lack of trust in the criminal justice system.

According to the 2012 FBI crime estimate, the number of reported forcible rapes per 100,000 people in the state of Rhode Island is 27.4%, with 288 victims and Connecticut at 25.6%, with 919 victims. The state of Alaska had the highest rate 57.2%. Do you know how your state rates on this horrific crime against both men and women?

How can we as a society change the mind-set of those who do not believe, "No" means "No"?

NOTE: statistics taken from the FBI website

To Be Loved

You have a choice, you can say *no* when given an invitation to a play, a dance or dinner, but what choice did Paul have? He was not given the chance to say no, he was not invited, he was trapped by the word, the word I found so hard to say ... *RAPE*. Was it fair of me to trap him in this horror I called my world?

For the next five months as I continued therapy, the lid to Pandora's box became ajar as memories surfaced. Ms. Zest had encouraged me to spend more time with Paul, as I felt most safe when I was with him. Also, I was able to relax enough to sleep. I spent every weekend with Paul and soon forgot those awful words he had spoken; however he could not forget mine. The intimacy we once shared was tainted and no matter how calm my body was at the end of the evening, the night would always close with the same horror. This crazy lady would be rocking, crying and yelling, all curled up on the floor and Paul would be trying to control the moment and bring her back to reality. In time he would succeed and tuck her back into bed. Safe in his arms, I lay there silently, ashamed and humiliated, for I am that crazy lady and I just want my life back again.

One night as we lay in bed wrapped in each other's arms, my thoughts were clear and focused on Paul. There were faint shadows from the outdoors casting images onto the empty walls and the light from the moon danced on his skin. My desire to be as one was so intense that my body ached and my heart sang silently ... "I love you so much, I want you desperately." This pain of desire was causing my body to thrust in motion, my mouth watered, and the hunger for our erotic passions heightened. Tonight everything will be perfect, love flows through my blood and our bodies sing in rhythmic melody. And as I stared into Paul's eyes he did not say a word, but the words once spoken echo in my head, "Mary, do you know we have never had sex ... we've always made love." These words he spoke long ago. I'm intoxicated by his sweet scent, his mouth is warm as a baby's bath on my flesh and we are almost one. Our kisses of sweet saliva and volcanic eruptions are in the forecast and the taste of his salty sweat gives pleasure to my tongue. In my mind I'm thinking, "Hold on, Mary, you can do this." I'm almost there!

Oh, no! I lost my focus and the image of Paul fades and Tony takes his form and I begin to fight, scream and punch. "Get off me, get off me, let me go!"   And the nightmares appear all over again. Rocking and crying on the floor again. Oh, God I hate this ... please wash it away. The tears, the pain, wash it all away; it's like a cancer eating my spirit. I just want to be okay, to be sane again. Where is the old Mary?

Once again Paul has controlled the moment and brought me back to reality and tucked me back into bed. "Hit me with your best shot!" That's what he said. How could I do that? I punched Paul square in the jaw but I don't remember doing it. My erotic desire, this passion of love, had turned to fear and fear turned to rage, then tears turned to shame. As I lay there in his arms with my face resting on his cushion of chest hair, I was scared. Where was this rage coming from? I felt so fragile, like a china doll. But this china doll had fallen from the shelf and I feared that no glue on earth could fix her.

I heard somewhere that art therapy was gaining widespread use in the treatment of patients suffering from trauma, so I decided to enroll in an art class. As I walked into the classroom for the first time, not sure what to expect, I was greeted by Mandy Falk, the artist and instructor. This middle-aged, slender, German, with shoulder-length bronze hair and green eyes expressed compassion for her students. It was a small class of about ten students, some dealing with cancer, some physical abuse, some death, and then there was me. I never admitted my reasons for participating in this class. Mandy would assign a project to be completed on our own time to be shared at the next class. She suggested the purchase of a book to be used as a journal for the art projects. Our first assignment was to place our feelings about our personal issues on paper.

That night as I lay in bed thinking of this project, all that came to mind was a scene from my childhood. I was about five years old, running down the sidewalk and falling, scraping my knees. There were tiny pebbles embedded under the skin and my mother had to dig them out. Oh, how it hurt! I remember screaming and trying to get away from my mother but she just held me down and kept digging in my knee. Then the image of being pricked in my hand by the needles of the pine Christmas tree came to the forefront of my memories and I could smell the fragrance of the pine. In the morning after breakfast, having those thoughts in mind, I grabbed my journal and some glue, then went outside to start my project. It took all of ten minutes and I was done, having covered the page with glue, sprinkled with gravel from the driveway and to top it off, added a few pine needles from the front trees in Paul's yard. Yes, this was exactly how I felt … I had been dragged through a gravel bank and then across a field of pine trees with the force of a tornado and the remains of the needles can still be found under my skin. What I had heard about art therapy was correct, for me this was a powerful experience and one that I would encourage anyone with deep-rooted issues to take advantage of.

It's hard work, this constant struggle to stay sane and recover from the past, so I turn to my Bible and my poetry; together with this art journal I find comfort and know I am not alone. Remembering the passages from "Footprints":

One night a man had a dream. He dreamed he was walking along the beach with the Lord. Across the sky flashed scenes from his life. For each scene, he noticed two sets of footprints in the sand; one belonged to him, and the other to the Lord.

When the last scene of his life flashed before him, he looked back at the footprints in the sand. He noticed that many times along the path of his life there was only one set of footprints. He also noticed that it happened at the very lowest and saddest times in his life.

This really bothered him and he questioned the Lord about it. "Lord, you said that once I decided to follow you, you'd walk with me all the way. But I have noticed that during the most troublesome times in my life, there is only one set of footprints. I don't understand why when I needed you most you would leave me."

The Lord replied, "My precious, precious child, I love you and I would never leave you. During your times of trial and suffering, when you see only one set of footprints, it was then that I carried you."

***

It was now late September and the weather was perfect for camping. With all this diverse therapy I was feeling stronger and it seemed only natural to move forward one step. So, with Paul's help, I had set up my campsite at Burlingame State Campground in Charlestown, Rhode Island. This was a campsite for one and I was the only one to reside here. As Paul drove away, uneasiness started to creep in, but this time I was in control. This was not the first time I had kindled a campfire here. In my former marriage we were avid campers, spending many weekends with the children in these very woods. Besides, camping today is not the same as camping fifty years ago when you were deep in the woods alone with no other campers in sight. Today camping is pitching a tent next to your neighbor; he's only a scream away.

That night after the campfire was smothered out, I prepared myself for a safe night's sleep by placing a flashlight under my pillow and just for added protection, one very sharp knife still in the case was placed next to it. As I lay down for the night I began to adjust and readjust the knife to make sure it was in reach, just in case there was an intruder. It took a while for my eyes to adjust to the darkness and the cool damp air. Then lights from cars driving past my campsite gave way to shadows through the canvas. The sleep I experienced this night was that of a new mother whose ears are on high alert, listening for the cries of her newborn and I was woken by cries from outside my tent. They were cries from a young child. There was no time to make a plan, this child needed help.

I bolted from the air mattress, wearing only Paul's T-shirt, and grabbed the flashlight, then quickly unzipped the tent door and headed straight toward the cries. At the edge of the road in front of my campsite, I could see clearly two figures next to the tree. A young scared girl about the age of seven was pressed up against the tree crying, and this man was leaning over her and yelling. "Mary…don't panic; Mary, don't panic"; these words I repeated to myself as I knelt down next to her. She needed me and she was my only concern. "Are you okay?" I asked. With tearful eyes she looked at me and said, "No, I want to go home, I want to talk to my mother, he won't let me talk to my mother."

At this point I was stroking the little girl's hair and rubbing her arms and hands in an attempt to comfort her. I turned to the man and asked, "Who are you and where is her mother?" He explained that the girl was his child and he was divorced, this was his custody weekend and they were camping with his friends. He then informed me that this outing was not going to be upset by calls to her mother. As we spoke I picked up the child in my arms and held her tight, then looked at that precious face and said, "You and I will go to the pay phone, we will call your mother." Then turning to the father who didn't know what to make of me and my boldness, I told him he needed to realize the trauma his daughter must be undergoing from having her family torn apart. I added my feeling that she was the important one here and that his utmost concern should be for her. I don't know which word struck him but he said, "You are right, I love my daughter; you are right, I have a cell phone at the campsite and we will call her mother."

Gently we transferred the child from my arms to his and as he walked away, we exchanged smiles and the words "Thank you" came from his mouth. Turning away and walking toward my tent, I was very proud of myself for being so brave but more so for playing a positive role in changing someone's life. I was confident that her father would follow through with his promise.

In my tent again, and very tired, I lay down and tucked myself in for the night; sleep had captured me and I was not resisting. Noise outside the tent woke me again. At first I thought it was an animal but large shadows appeared on the wall of the tent. There were crunching sounds of something moving through the leaves and I could feel the vibrations in the earth beneath me from every step that landed on its surface. My eyes focused on this shadow and followed it as this mysterious creature from the dark circled my tent. Where was that brave lady who had just stood outside confronting a stranger in the night? How could she abandon me now?

Paralysis set in, I could not move, I could not speak and I tried so hard to move my hands, to grab that knife hidden under my pillow. Frozen by fear,-- it was more than fear; it was terror that I was going to be attacked again and I was not going to be able to protect myself. "Lord, protect me, please protect me, don't let this happen to me again, please, Lord." Over and over these words I chanted in my mind. I have no recollection of falling asleep but morning came and I opened my eyes; the Lord had protected me.

The air was still and the first sounds were that of the birds singing in the trees, then voices whispering from the nearby campsites and the aroma of freshly perked coffee penetrated the fabric of my tent. Just like a television commercial for Maxwell House coffee, it's the taste to wake up to. I tossed the blanket to one side, reached for the zipper on the door flap, unzipped the door and peeked outside. The sun had risen, many campers were up and about and it was time for me to join the population. Slipping on an old pair of gray sweat pants, socks and sneakers, I was off to the bath house to shower.

As I approached the building my attention was drawn to a small figure dressed in red pajamas, standing at the water fountain. Was this the little girl from last night? As I came closer she glanced my way and from nowhere her father appeared. The aura reflecting from both father and daughter was warm and friendly and they walked hand in hand toward me. The little blonde-haired girl looked up at me and said, "My father wants to say something to you." He and I were standing face to face on friendly ground and I knew he had kept his promise. We exchanged first names and then he said, "I can't thank you enough for all you did last night for both me and my daughter. I am so happy you were there and my daughter will be okay from now on." A few more words were shared, then we went our separate ways. As I walked away, the image of me standing in only a T-shirt entertained me for a moment and I wondered, given the traumatic events of that night, if he had even noticed. The weekend was now over and the camping experience had empowered me. I embraced this newly found power and returned home.

The days during the week dragged and I eagerly welcomed the weekends that I spent away from my mother's home as she had noticed changes in my behavior and the interrogations began. She was woken many nights by horrifying screams that generated from the room above her bedroom, the same screams that have awoken me. They are real and not just in my dreams as Ms. Zest thought, it wasn't in my mind, these were genuine. Bolting from her bed as I had done on the camping weekend, up the stairs ran my mother to rescue her little girl. Opening my eyes to my own screams, I knew the vision was real and this time it was my mother leaning over me. In panic she reached out to me and I pushed her away. "Mary, Mary, what's wrong, what happened? Are you okay?" She repeated, "Are you okay?" How do I keep my secret from her now? What do I say? "I'm okay, Mother, it was just a bad dream, go back downstairs, I'm okay now." And with that being said, she went back downstairs, and my secret had not been exposed.

This was a close call, but not as close as the night the grandchildren, Michael and Fallon, had stopped me in my tracks with their yells, "What's wrong, Grandma?" The children had spent the night and were sleeping downstairs on the living room floor. My eyes were wide open, and I was in a panic mode, screaming as I ran down the stairs, heading straight for the front door. I almost escaped when the children, woken by my screams, started to yell at me. The sound of their voices brought me back to reality and I replied, "Nothing's wrong, it's all right, go back to sleep." Then turning in embarrassment, I walked back upstairs to my bedroom and sat on the edge of the bed.

I am remembering another night I was alone in the house and found myself waking from sleep, screaming. As I opened my eyes, he was staring down at me. Utter fear took hold as I bolted from my bed. I remember putting my arms up as to push him away, then I found myself running from my room down the stairs, unable to stop running. When I opened the front door to continue this race across the front lawn, my heart was pounding faster and faster with each step. Before my legs could stop the motion, this fear had planted itself in the soles of my feet. How far would I run to escape?

As one foot hit the ground it was as if it was landing on springs; as the power surged downward, my foot was propelled up again. One up, one down, one up, one down, again and again. Were my feet trying to keep up with the beating of my heart? I did not feel the rough surface under my feet and I could only see a strange fog in front of me as I ran for my life. All I could think was to run, run as fast as I could, to get away from him. At times my aura felt his invasion of my safe zone and then I couldn't recognize my own heartbeat. Was he that close behind that I could hear his breath? Was my mind controlling this race?

Then suddenly a light came into sight, headlights from a car turning into my road and the light broke my state of altered consciousness. Startled, I swung my arms in my defense but there was no one there but me, standing in just my nightshirt in the cool of the night, alone, and in somewhat of a shock, knowing now that someone had just seen me standing on the road in my nightshirt at this ungodly hour of the night. I didn't want to be a statistic ... crazy lady found running through the streets of Westerly in her nightshirt.

Once panic retreated, I turned and started my journey back up the street to my house. Now, the pain set in with each step up this rough pavement. The night seemed even darker then before and strange sounds echoed from the woods. Was it a fox? Was it a deer? My internal compass led me up the street, one painful step at a time. By now, I could feel every stone or twig under my feet and it hurt. My aura was on alert, but thankfully it did not detect an intruder and my body began to relax as houses appeared in the foreground.

I did not know what time it was. Limping up the street, I noticed street lights flickering and the sounds I heard now were non-threatening. My body was starting to shiver and the perspiration of the night's events started to chill my flesh. Partway up the street an outside light went on and I noticed a sound, a neighbor letting his dog out on a run and giving him instruction to "Hurry, do your business, it's cold out here." Like a statue standing stiff in the night, I stood frozen, not wanting to be seen. The dog barked and chased a cat as it ran past him, heading in my direction. Luckily for me the beagle was stopped abruptly by the tug of his collar at the end of his run. One might have thought the cat was after the bats flying so low in the night air. Soon his master reeled him in and the lights went out and I was safe to continue my journey up the street again. "Oh, Lord, please don't let anyone see me, please." Once inside my house, resting on the sofa, my thoughts flashed back to this night's horror and how real it all seemed. One thing was certain--my feet were bleeding and all torn-up ... that was real.

It's early October now, the air is crisp but I am unable to breathe, feeling stifled and needing to escape from everything and everyone, everyone! My thoughts are torn in multiple directions, so many decisions I must come to terms with. Paul has plans this weekend and now I am sentenced to a weekend at home, my home, with my mother and with my nightmares. The forty-five minute drive from the casino to the driveway of mother's home allows for plans of my own to be plotted on this cool Friday evening ... my escape. Imprisonment in this house of nightmares was not in my plan.

As I walked into the house, mother was waiting as usual with many questions, for this was the highlight of her day. She loves me and, like a lonely spouse, every night as I arrive home, she is there to open the door and steal away all my attention – but not tonight. "Mary, how was your day? Did your boss give you a hard time?" Her opening remarks are etched in my memory. "My day was the usual, same old, same old. I'm in a hurry, got to pack my bags, I'm going away for the weekend." This was my answer. Then abruptly I ran up the stairs to avoid further questioning, such as, "What do you mean, going away for the weekend?"

Where would I tell her I was going? I wasn't sure myself. All I knew was that I was leaving, driving away on an adventure, wherever the road would lead, anyplace was better than here. From my bedroom, yelling into the air, "Mother, it's Friday and I just have to get away." Guilt plagued my words, how could I get away without lying to her, without hurting her feelings? I told myself I didn't need her permission for this trip. The first item tossed into my travel bag, in order of importance to me, was my Bible, second was my favorite poetry book, *The Portable Oscar Wilde*, then a swimsuit, a few items of clothing and a heavy coat. Oh, yes, I mustn't forget the address book and maps of Rhode Island, Connecticut and Massachusetts. By know I was gasping for breath with anticipation of the unknown and like the camping trip, this adventure would serve me well.

Time to face mother. Talking to myself as I walked down the stairs, head held high, "Mary, do this for yourself. You need to find yourself ... just do it." At the bottom of the landing she stood, and with her sad, steel-blue eyes stared at me. Then, avoiding the truth, I placed a kiss on her cheek and never replied to her question, "Guess you won't be back home from Paul's until Monday?" Mother had just comforted me, no need to lie, she granted my escape by her words, "Guess you won't be back from Paul's until Monday?" As I walked out the door heading to my car I yelled out, "See you on Monday. Mother, have a nice weekend and keep out of trouble and call Bill if you need anything. I love you."

I stepped into the car and as my derrière rested against the seat, my lungs expanded and my rib cage inflated, and as I inhaled, like a prisoner taking his first breath of freedom, I exhaled and waved bye to mother and made my escape. Heading north on Route 95 as daylight faded, the lights from the oncoming cars nearly blinded my vision as traffic bottlenecked in certain sections, then loosened up again to allow the flow of vehicles. Tractor-trailers appeared from nowhere as the night unfolded. Click, click, thump, thump, the melody of classical music accompanied the lyrics from traveling vehicles, drums beating from far away. No, not drums but growls emerging from my stomach, as the internal dinner bell announced with authority, "Find food, time to eat."

Was I stupid, brave or adventurous? Did it matter? This jail-bird had flown the coop and landed in Plymouth, Massachusetts, and I settled into my room in a very delightful hotel equipped with swimming pool and hot tub. Yes, destination was found. The sensation of butterflies fluttering in my tummy tickled my very spirit and laughter erupted from within as the reflection in the mirror testified, "I did it, freedom is mine."

It was grand, only myself to think about, no one knew me so I could act childish if I chose and I chose to. On Saturday morning I took a walk into the park by the pond. Families of mallard ducks were swimming back and forth and turtles were basking on the warm rocks at the edge of the water. It appeared that the park's maintenance crew had raked autumn leaves in piles to be vacuumed up at a later date. Lucky for me as I had found a hefty pile to lie in and, placing my handbag under my head as a pillow, I closed my eyes to listen to nature's sounds and enjoy the warmth of the sun's rays on my face.

Pretending I was blind, I tested my senses to evaluate the ones I could rely on, then realized the fact was that they were in competition. As I inhaled deeply, the musty smell of decaying leaves stimulated my sense of smell and birds singing in nearby trees echoed in my ear, entertaining my thoughts. The bed of leaves beneath massaged my body with vibrations of every pounding footstep. The sense of time was for yesterday as I had removed my watch earlier and tucked it away in my handbag – there was no time schedule and I would only live for the moment.

My afternoon was spent in the swimming pool floating in the water, sometimes with my eyes closed, then open, to stare at the decorative ceiling tiles, always in tune with the movement of the water and comparing myself to an embryo in the womb. Late afternoon was my time to reflect and read the Bible or a few poems and by nightfall I would order from room service, my favorite a pizza and a couple of beers. For some, my weekend away might have seemed boring but for me it was spiritual and energizing and on my return trip home I was much more focused and at peace.

Fear

As teenagers, my cousin Tim and I would sit in chairs opposite each other and stare into each other's eyes, focusing into the pupil, faces stern, no expressions and bodies motionless. This game we played and soon it became a skill, and I could out stare him, drawing energy from his soul. If the opportunity presented itself, I would take advantage of young and old in a challenge of minds, knowing I would prevail.

Once the memories of the rape surfaced, I was no longer able to stare into that black hole of another's soul. Now when confronted in conversations with both men and women, my eyes would stray, scanning their facial appearance, the mouth, ears, nose, hairstyle and their sense of fashion, never pausing for that snapshot of their eyes. There was a definite difference in my behavior and mannerisms that had become quite noticeable, so noticeable that one of my female friends began commenting on it.

"Why does your head drop forward and why are you grasping your hands, twisting your fingers when we talk? What's bothering you?" Of course I would just blow it off and say, "I didn't notice!" But, I did notice and I wasn't able to control that reflex to look away. This voice inside my head was a constant reminder of the dangers of the world. Would I see the rapture in his eyes? Should I be afraid of him, too? Danger! Danger all around me!

One Saturday morning in early October 2001, as I was walking down the frozen food section in our local supermarket, a slightly overweight, bearded fellow approached my carriage. Not realizing at first that it was John, a coworker and friend from many years past, in the days of pre-divorce, and trials and tribulations during the early stages of my divorce. John would bring in comfort foods such as chocolate to share. It wasn't just chocolates we shared; we shared war stories of his divorce and our common interest in flying. John is a pilot and was restoring historical planes and I had been in the Civil Air Patrol as a teen and had received instructions in flight. I have always wished a pilot's license had been obtained, but dating boys soon became my priority.

The sight of his smile brought back recollections of better days and the camaraderie between us. John reached out to embrace and likewise I held his hug just airspace enough away not to be noticed. In conversation John mentioned he had accumulated credit hours enough for two one-hour flights in a World War II fighter plane. Light glowing from envy brightened my face, and open mouth insert foot, "Well, lucky you!" OOPS! What was I saying? John's reply caught me very much off guard, I wasn't expecting an invitation to fly off into the sunset for 'free.' But only fools turn down an opportunity such as this one. I was not a fool!

John arrived early the next morning at my house, my mother's home, then off to Quonset Point Naval Base, stopping along the way for takeout coffee and muffins. Jeeps aren't the smoothest riding vehicles, one sudden bump and coffee went flying; no, this wasn't a trial run. Visualizing the cockpit windows closing and me strapped down into the seat was a bit unnerving; I had forgotten how claustrophobic I had become over these past few years. But I couldn't turn back now and after all I wasn't that uncomfortable in John's company ... this was a good thing!

Movie stars we are about to be. There are video cameras attached to the wings, outside the front window, and at the back window. And there is a remote inside the cockpit so we can control all the cameras and capture fluctuations in our voices, sights and sounds to remember. Our pilots were from Australia and their purpose was to guide the plane's takeoff and landing and of course, act as film crew when needed.

Hallelujah, we were told there was no need to close the cockpit and I was resting easier in the front seat now that my claustrophobia was in check. Do you know how free one feels up in the clouds? As I stared down over the wing to the earth below, the freedom of this flight was breathtaking. The landscape below was of a patchwork quilt, every scene well planned by the craftsman of design. I was enjoying my control of this plane, banking to the right, backing to the left, keeping level with the horizon. John was flying above my plane and banking to the right, dipped into a roller coaster spin and leveled off again just to fly upside down.

From where I sat my view was clear, no obstructions, as my Australian co-pilot joked from behind and I was almost drawn in by his accent. Noah was extremely attractive, maybe in his mid-forties, and had a body like a "Chip and Dale" dancer. Yes, there are some things you notice no matter how distracted you may be. Did he think I was not as daring as John? My flight consisted of right and left banks and a few slight nose dives and then holding the control stick firmly pulling towards my chest we would travel toward the heavens. It wasn't long into the flight that those fears took hold, just when I was feeling so free and at one with the heavens. At least Noah was seated behind me and would never see the expression on my face, I thought. But, that quiver in my voice, well, he didn't know me so he might just think it was normal.

Apparently Noah's perception was right on target as he asked "Are you scared? Your voice sounds a little shaky; you don't have to do any stunt you are uncomfortable doing. If you like I can take over." "No, I'm okay, it'll be just a few more minutes and I'll relax. I can't wait to get this video and show off my flying to my son Rob. He will just envy me. He took a few flying lessons as a teen and planned on attending Embry and Riddle flight school in Florida after graduation from high school, but he never followed that dream."

We shared constant chatter through the intercom from one topic to another; I was attempting to control the fear through conversation and praying that Noah would respect my air space – hands off, "Oh, Lord, please don't let him reach out to touch my shoulders." The hour was almost over and as Noah took control, I agreed to a rollover. Yes, let's do it again – this brought back the tingling sensations I felt in my tummy as a child as my father drove fast up to the top of this very steep hill then, just before the descent, over one bump, then down the hill. With the sudden impact over the bump we children were airborne, laughing, yelling, "Do it again, Daddy."

Smooth landing, once on the ground, out of the plane and I was given the canisters of film and the video. We said our good-byes and John drove me home. Another outing conquered successfully, fear surrendered, and I carried the day with a smile.

There are those who cannot be read easily, not I! If there is excitement brewing inside, the joy in my heart illuminates my facial expressions. Likewise, words are unspoken but secrets are told through these dances of expression.

Common ground must be shared and now there was a reason for a visit to Connecticut. Rob was my second son, he and Bill were born just twelve months apart. Unlike Bill, Rob was born with blonde-hair and blue eyes. Standing on the porch about to ring the doorbell, all these emotions came to surface, then suddenly the door opened. Rob greeted me at the door with hugs and as I went to kiss his cheek, his coarse beard scratched my face. As we sat down on the living room sofa to play the video, my main objective was to watch his every expression intently. Would he be as excited to see me in control as I was to hear his words of approval?

Role reversal has come into play these past years and it is I seeking approval and guidance from my son Rob. Gone are the days of rearing children with a firm hand – his wife has that delightful responsibility. Yes, I was met with approval, there was excitement in Rob's voice as he asked questions and commented, "That's my mom flying." As our eyes took in the sights and sounds, those recognizable sounds of tremor surrounding every spoken word were heard, and Rob joked, "Mom, feeling a bit scared, are we?" Another outing conquered successfully -- wrong!

I wasn't able to claim that accomplishment this time. The news broadcasters are famous for airing personal interest stories where the public happens to be at the right spot at the right time with video in hand, incriminating or embarrassing moments "caught on video." This was that moment caught in time, visions of distortions, and my facial expressions were tattooed with terror and recorded for future reference, a constant reminder of this trauma. My attacker has robbed all joy and even in the shadows of heaven he waits.

Wash It Away

The weekends spent with Paul were now including nights in midweek and if I could, I would never leave. His home has become my personal spa, a place for both body and spirit to be pampered and nurtured. It's now late October, the air is crisp, and leaves are falling from the trees. Jack o'lanterns are displayed on many front porches and soon we will participate in the rituals of Halloween. These are happy times, new and pleasant memories are being created. I haven't been to a Halloween party in years; the last one I can remember was when I was twelve years old and at the age of fifty-one, the excitement of dressing up in costume still intrigued me. Paul went as Count Dracula and I his bride … a far cry from the Cinderella story, but for me the ending was a happy one.

Time waits for no man and the turning of months, a chill is in this 2001 November air and the clouds hint of snow. This morning, at home, there is a twist in the daily routine; I am curled up on the floor in my bedroom, in a puddle of blood, the color of red on the tips of my fingers. The demons are back and this time their claws have attacked from inside, inside those private parts that are no more. Red as fire, dripping from within and the pain of scars lingers for hours. In denial of this vision before me, I walk to the bathroom and step into the shower, cleanse myself, then return to my room and clear away all evidence of this vile act. Oh Lord, what have I done? Did I attempt to cut myself?

In today's art class we are to paint whatever comes to the surface, don't plan it out, just let the emotions of the moment guide our strokes. Over the past few weeks the emotions have run freely and colors signify my characters, green for the attacker, yellow for Paul, the color of my favorite rose, and red the color of the stop sign on the street corner ... that was me.

With abstract strokes of color my hand guided the brush across the twenty-four by thirty-six-inch piece of paper; stroke by stroke, layer by layer, until all was covered. Mandy had given instructions that for no reason were our eyes to stray to observe those around us. "Heads down," she said. Standing far in the back corner, she was able to observe her students, their reactions or lack of them. Like a river flowing downstream, tears flowed from my eyes, down my face and landed on my painting.

With every stroke, emotions unleashed, tears flowed and the pressure of my hand on the brush increased. At one point the sound of pounding could be heard as I whipped the brush again and again into the many layers of color; higher and higher in the air my arm would stretch out with rage, then suddenly someone grabbed my arm and stopped me. It was Mandy. Afraid to look up, afraid the whole class would be staring, I felt her gently touch my face as if to tilt it her way. I looked up to be met with eyes of compassion; she did not judge me. She just said, "Mary, I can see that was so painful for you. Do you know what I want you to do?" And I answered, "No, what should I do?"

Then she proceeded to lay out the next step in this project. I was told to choose one color and cover the entire painting, don't leave any evidence of the original strokes. "No, I can't do that!" Without thinking these were the words from my mouth. Mandy gave me this reassuring look and said, " Wash it away, wash it away and you will feel much better." So, black was the color, black as the night which demons roam, the first stroke of the brush was the most difficult. Again, layer by layer, stroke by stroke, washing away those painful shades of green and this time when tears rolled down my cheeks, they too sang the song, wash away, wash away, wash away all.

The anger was gone and the tears dried up; I was calm, relaxed and very tired. How did she know I would feel such a healing effect once the painting was washed away? Mandy, standing behind me, placed her hands on my shoulders and with gentle movements across each shoulder, moved down my back with the palm of her hand with just the right pressure to release the tension beneath. She didn't need to say anything for she knew I was in a different place now. Class was over and as we gathered our materials, one student walked toward me and, placing her hand on my arm, she said, "You are so deep, it seems to be easy for you to express your emotions." I just smiled and walked out the door.

On the drive home I couldn't stop thinking of Mandy and about those words she spoke, "Wash it away." Where had I heard them before? Oh, I remember where it was, our very first class, in Mandy's introduction and the video was part of her presentation. As we were sitting in chairs lined in rows facing the screen just like a movie theater, she turned off the lights and turned on the video. It was a documentary about art therapy and the effects this process has played in the recovery of trauma victims. Some were cancer survivors, others had lost their loved ones in violent crimes. As the story unfolded, many survivors shared their traumas and how the art therapy played a large role in their recovery. As one survivor put it, "Wash it away. Just paint your life story, the traumatic event that brought you to this class, then the finishing touch would be to *wash it away.*" I watched as she, with a bucket of solution and scrub brush, washed months of emotions from these canvases. Others just washed it away by painting over the canvas with a single color. As I sat there watching the video, I wondered how could they just destroy these beautiful pieces of art. I remember how bravely she spoke as she said, "And now I'm in a different place."

Today is Thanksgiving and Paul and I enjoyed a quiet day, just the two of us at his house. Paul was doing the cooking, a small turkey with the trimmings and I was relaxing on the sofa. Laughter was echoing from the living room as I was watching old reruns of the Three Stooges, and Paul commented on the pleasant sounds my laughter made. I was never one to laugh out loud but these days I was and I also enjoyed the sound of my laughter. I can sense restlessness in Paul and the realization that our days together will soon come to an end. He never turns me away but sometimes rushes me out the door and one day this door will close behind me, never to open again. I will have a safe haven when this day comes as I have signed a contract and construction of my very own home will start soon.

Life is okay, work is going well, and I'm making great progress in my sessions with Ms. Zest. She and I have discussed in depth my progress in art therapy and my detaching from Paul. I know in my heart this is the right thing to do, he can no longer help me. It's not healthy for me to stay here and subconsciously pretend I am his bride. We agree, I must walk away from this relationship with Paul, but the only question remains, when? Soon it will be December and the Christmas holiday, maybe it's an excuse but the timing is not right and to be honest, just because I know it's the right thing to do, doesn't mean I truly want to follow through with it. Saying good-bye, letting go of my first love, my only love, who would blame me for hanging on just a while longer?

The temperature has dropped and snowflakes melt then freeze and turn to ice. This is the weather you expect for the first week of December. This evening I'm running behind schedule, going to be late for my art class; not only late, but forgot my materials at home and there is no time to turn around and go back. There are two ways to get into the studio: one you go down the alleyway between the buildings to the walkway along the water and into the entrance. The second way is to cut through the Old Loran Building, go down one level, out the back door onto the walkway and the studio door is right there. I always take the second way, it's safer. This night was no different but when I walked through the back door and it closed, there was a click and the door locked behind me. In addition the door to the studio was locked and a sign "No Class Tonight" was taped to the window.

This was not news to me, I had just forgotten. The walkway was covered in ice and holding the railing so as not to slip and fall, I started my journey. But before I could walk more than a few steps there was a noise coming from the alleyway. In my mind this meant only one thing and just like the night in the tent I froze; the signals from my brain were not being received by my legs and my feet would not move. What will I do? How will I protect myself if someone is there?

As I glanced over the railing at the water below, it looked so cold and the current was moving swiftly by. My first thought was to climb over the metal fence and jump into the river; if I was lucky I would not drown. Death was more welcoming to me then meeting up with a stranger in the dark. I'd rather die than have someone touch me again. Now I had a plan. Then the noise stopped and silence filled the air. The magnet that held my feet in place on this icy walkway had released just enough so I could slide one foot, then the other, in slow motion across the cold wet surface. Holding the railing and pulling with my hands down to the end of the walkway, the sounds of my heart beating and racing in time echoed in my ears.

Now confronted with the turn into the alleyway, I had no railings to hold onto and I knew this would be a struggle. Chanting out loud, "Lord help me, Lord help me, please help me." As I chanted I could feel my feet move a little more and just a little more until that last step, and I was free on the sidewalk out on the main street in front of the Old Loran Building. I knew if I looked back there would only be one set of footsteps and I gave thanks to the Lord for carrying me out to safety.

Christmas is but a week away and Ms. Zest has scheduled this pre-holiday session and boy do I need this one. After the experience on the waterfront at the art studio, there was another frightful experience on the table at my electrologist's office. We Italian hairy women are vain creatures and unwanted hair must be attacked and destroyed no matter what the cost. My mother and sisters have used some sort of hair removal system for years. First it was trimming these fine long dark brown hairs above the lip and then, as the hairs grew in thicker, waxing was introduced. It didn't sound as though anyone was enjoying this process, first apply hot wax to your flesh followed by screams. Hot! Hot! And after it dries prepare yourself for even more discomfort as mother, standing over you ever so proud with delight in her eyes, would pull the cold wax off your face as quickly as possible. But the end result was always the same, hair removal with ... pain.

Were my sisters masochistic and did my mother enjoy their songs of pain sung out of tune? "That's okay, mom, my mustache doesn't bother me, I'll just cover it with makeup. Other girls in school have face hair." This was my reply to her invitation and in time she gave up her quest to remove my faint mustache. My interest was piqued when electrolysis was introduced and for the past ten years I've had almost painless intermittent treatments to remove hair.

I had just a slight shadow on my upper lip but with Christmas approaching and Paul's Christmas party this weekend, I was off to the electrologist for a treatment to zap away this faint masculine image. After I climbed onto the table and was lying on my back, Ann my electrologist, who was ten years my senior, placed pillows under my thighs, knees and neck, so I was comfortable during the treatment. We chatted as she pulled this large magnifying glass which hung from a hinge on the wall into place above my face then she placed goggles over my eyes. "Relax, Mary." Words spoken in a soft voice as she caressed my right hand, placing lotion into the palm and then a metal grounding bar. "Okay Mary, grasp the bar gently, are you comfortable? I'm ready to start." My usual reply, "All set." In the background meditation music was playing, and when I inhaled, the fragrance of lavender filled my senses. With warm gentle hands, Ann tilted my face to the right and then re-positioned the pillow under my neck to slightly under my shoulders, allowing my head to rest against the edge of the table.

Midway through the process of zapping hairs the sensation of mosquitoes snacking at my face gave way to inner emotions as my body uncontrollably reacted. Legs stiffened and toes posed ballerina style as if both legs were strapped together and if my body had been placed upright, I would be standing on my toes waiting for the audience applause to begin. The goggles covering my eyes acted as a dam until the pressure gave way and the salty tears streamed down my cheeks.

With arms of a solder straight by my sides and fists gripped so tight that nail marks almost drew blood, the arch of my back rose to meet the ceiling, leaving only the tip of my head touching the table – body distorted. Frozen in time, visions of me being held down with force, visions of the rape, had paralyzed my movements and I could not feel the tenseness of the clinch of my teeth. What's happening to me, am I having a seizure? What triggered this dance of distortion? Was it Ann's soft voice or the heat of her breath against my face as she worked the needle into the hair follicles? It seemed as though this distortion lasted for ten minutes and I was afraid that some permanent damage would be the results.

"Mary, what's the matter?" Ann kept repeating. In her voice I could hear concern as she stroked my face and arms then lightly massaged my feet and legs. The only reaction to her efforts to calm my body were my mere nodding of my head, then cries and finally I was able to speak out, "I'm sorry, Ann, I'm sorry." Ann and I had shared conversations but I had never exposed my life traumas with her and this was not the time to open up. She was my electrologist, not my friend, and I'm humiliated enough by this horror show I just performed; if only I could erase this past hour.

"Mary, you've had a hard life, I can tell. You poor thing. You must take care ... a massage would help. A cranial-sacral massage – I know you're concerned about the money but you really should be thinking about your health now and well, let's get you relaxed first, then I'll talk about it. "The transition from bodily stiffness to relaxation was bridged first with moments of cold shakes and finally exhaustion. Once able to sit up and leave for home, I walked, walked ... walked as fast as my legs would carry me, right out that door, leaving this humiliation behind. Why does my body react so instinctively? I guess it's just the healing process.

Well, what was Ms. Zest thinking? At the end of our pre-Christmas session we both agreed I should be proud of my progress and the control I had taken on the waterfront. So many feelings and memories were opening, Ms. Zest suggested it might help if I were to read materials on rape, but of course I refused. "I'm not ready to read anything like that. No crying today, guess I am making progress." Then we hugged as usual, saying our good-byes and Ms. Zest says, "Mary, have a nice Christmas and I'll see you in a few weeks." Walking toward the door I turned to look back then smiled as if to say, "You, too," and I walked out the door. My goal now was to hurry back to Paul's house to help hang a wall tapestry.

My body is overloading with memories and emotions of detachments, demons, and a slithering worm. Her presence, the other woman, this slithering worm, invades my space at Paul's house and throughout all our shopping, buying furniture, decorating and the urgency to have everything completed by Christmas – my thoughts are of her. I feel I am doing all this just for her, for her benefit. As Paul stands on the ladder I give instructions, move it to the right. No, just a little higher, perfect! We were attempting to hang this beautiful twelve-foot ancient tapestry on the stairwell wall. I knew my days were numbered and as I stood on the landing, tugging on the metal bar in the hem of the tapestry, making last adjustments, silently this detachment began. Let's just get through Christmas and see what the New Year brings, my silent thoughts are that everything must be perfect for her.

This Too Will Pass

Every wardrobe should have a red sweater; you know, the one you wear during the Christmas season at least once. My mother and I are shopping for that red sweater, the one I will wear this year to my son Bill's for dinner on Christmas. Paul is traveling south to be with his family and should be back before the New Year.

Christmas morning Mom and I wasted no time and after dressing, we poured coffee into our travel mugs and off to Bill's for a late morning spread. He had reminded us to be there early to relax, snack and open gifts..........dinner would follow later. It was Bill's family, my son Chris and we in-laws and out-laws from both sides. You'd think that once divorced and children grown, holidays spent with your ex-spouse would be a thing of the past. Wrong! And somehow the seating arrangement always placed him at the head and me at his side. Oh, well it's only dinner and we are civil and at times just a bit more than civil; after all, there were twenty-eight Christmases together.

Christmas music playing in the background, candles burning, and Bill's home was dressed for the occasion with many brightly colored decorations adorning the walls. As I

stood in front of the Christmas tree searching for the orna-
ments I had given as gifts to them in years past, I could feel
my lips smiling as the many fond memories of those days
overwhelmed me. To the right of the tree I could see my
mother sitting there all comfy, for she is responsible for my
being, and as I glanced at my sons I thought, "And I am
responsible for their being." Of course then that makes them
responsible for the being of their children and so life goes on.
And with this thought I silently gave thanks to my Mother for
allowing me to be, after all it was her choice. Today we gather
to celebrate the birth of Jesus ... did anyone remember?

I carried the many packages while my son Bill helped
his Grandmother to the car. He lingered for a few moments to
give instructions on traveling, "Drive slow," he said. He
kissed his Grandmother on the cheek, and said, "I love you."
Then watching him walk around the car to my side, I press the
button and my window slowly rolls down, he leans his head
through the window and repeats the same words, "I love you,
Mom, be careful and drive slow, thanks for coming."
Mother and I engage in mindless chatter on the drive
home. I was preoccupied with the road conditions as we
began to slide; I was losing traction, but then gained control.
Sometimes I drive faster then I should, so mindful of this,
mother repeats Bill's words, "Be careful, Mary." I listen and
obey. It takes about thirty minutes to travel from Peace Dale
to Westerly and once on the back-roads you can really take in
the beauty of the crystal trees and the wires looped from pole
to pole heavy with ice. The snow on the roadside was
flawless, not soiled with prints of any kind. Mother mentioned
we could use music, so reaching in the side compartment, I
pulled out one of my favorite cassettes, "Yanni Snow Fall"
and within moments her request is granted.

Like sand in an hour glass, piled high, waiting to be released through the narrow passage to fall freely to the bottom, only to be tumbled around and repeat the endless journey over and over again, so was I.

Those days, tears were less frequent and casual conversation was more likely to be exchanged during my sessions with Ms. Zest, as the memories of that night of the rape have all surfaced. There was a party going on, a celebration hosted on Memory Island and the party favors from Pandora's box had been distributed to the guests. And when the party was over and the guests were gone, the only evidence of my celebration was this empty box and the mess left behind. I alone was the only cleaning crew who was capable of restoring the Island to some sense of order and in my own fashion the work began.

And in the fashion of art, my art, the mission of cleaning the island began. Sitting here among the other students in my art class, staring down at the box of pastels, I was at that very critical moment, the moment that would determine the future of the paper below. The soothing shade of light blue tempted my hand and I could not resist. With a soft stroke in curving motions, I started from the top left corner of the page, like an airplane in free flight landing at the bottom in the middle and gliding down the runway for just a few moments, only to pick up speed again and soar through the sky. With a swift stroke my hand was at the top of the page on the right corner and the puffs of blue smoke could be seen from afar ... the outline of this island.

What do I want for this painting? What do I want for my life? And with shades of green I draw ribbons tied to red balloons floating freely over the deep blue cold Atlantic Ocean and the crisp winter air encases my balloons and they are preserved for eternity. The vision is clear, I've answered my question. I am those red balloons, floating through the air, I do feel freer these day … I am healing, and those satin green ribbons gently tied to the folds of these balloons, once holding me down with weight, now added grace to my flight. The rape was dropped into the ocean but the memory, like the green ribbons, will tag along forever.

If the Atlantic Ocean was to the right, then the pounding surf echoing from the other side of the island must be the Pacific and as the tide rushes out to sea, all that's left of my love are those haunting eyes. And after drawing one very large warm, blue, compassionate eye, then I caress his lids in red and pray that he will always remember me, then with pastels of golden sun rays the finishing touches are added and Paul is set afloat to start his life again.

Then turning to the smoky blue outlined image in the middle of the page I proceed to complete this very emotional task which waits. This area of the island now resembles the forehead of a face and with a steady hand and firm grip, I carve the eyes of my attacker into the mountains that rise high in the sky. The pupil is colored in a soft shade of green as the hold he had on me is gone and I gain strength from this trauma so I color his iris red to symbolize my embrace. I must embrace this memory to be able to release it and move on.

The view from the mountain top is spectacular, and a cool mist from the waterfalls below fill the air, as the water splashes against the rocks below; I am one step closer to letting go. With a black charcoal in hand I repeated my strokes, back and forth, round and round this half circle until a solid mass covered this spot, this was the eye of the freezing cold black ledge of the waterfall. As the release of tears cleanses the spirit, so too does the flow of water; memories, tears tumble down, down the page in deep shades of red, green and yellow and as the bottom of the page nears, the shades begin to fade. And with the passage of time the pain is not as sharp and the memories not so clear. Class is over, and order was reinstated on Memory Island, as I pick up the mess, and place it back in Pandora's box.

Thoughts of the inevitable plagued me night and day and at times I even blamed Paul for the rape. Those cruel unbelievable words whispered in my ear, that deep haunting voice of my attacker, "The sex must be good," he said. "He's only with you because the sex must be good." He was referring to Paul. Paul was my salvation during the rape, that focal point I traveled to, it was his face I saw when I was being raped and now my thoughts were getting confused. If I had never dated Paul then I would not have been raped ... it's his fault.

There were times I felt abandoned by all the men in my life; my father stopped caressing me when I was going through puberty and my husband had broken his wedding vows before our first anniversary. Then my younger brother died in a car accident and left me, my sons grew up and other women replaced me and my first love could not surrender his love to me. Putting closure to events in our lives is healthy and important, you kill the "what if" and grow through the disappointments, and then you can grind your heels into the "here and now." And now here I am.....

The Inevitable Plagued Me

I've been tempting fate, mixing a cocktail or two with a dose of Paxil; I feel no different, and after all it is the holidays, but now it's a New Year. Happy New Year, 2002!

This day in February started out no different from any other visit to my son Bill's house, but the return trip home that night after a couple of glasses of wine, that detour to Paul's house, this inevitable plague that haunted me became my mission for the night. I was not drunk, I was happy, I was strong, I knew I could do this, I was ready … and to be honest, I wanted to do this.

As I drove down the road away from Peace Dale, practicing my words out load, just the right words to tell Paul I was moving on, letting him go, just want to be friends, I'm okay with you dating others, I began crying hysterically. It's normal I thought, I was mourning the death of a friend, a lover. Before me … I could see that gray metal casket lowering slowly down into the worm-filled earth below. This nauseating feeling in the pit of my stomach, this uncontrollable gagging reflex, the taste of bile was on my lips. And with a tissue in my right hand I wiped away the stench and with the left hand gripping the steering wheel as if to hang on for dear life, I turned into his driveway and the stage was set.

What happened next was like the scenes from a horror story and I was the leading lady. Do I believe in outer body experiences? What about being in two places at once or split personalities? I was never one hundred percent sure there was truth in any of this stuff until that night.

The view looking out from inside my car was a peaceful one, all was still on this landscaped wooded lot, the full moon in all its splendor high in the sky had cast a shadow on the snowy front yard below. The light from the living room windows of this two-story colonial was warm and welcoming. Was he home? His car was not in the driveway and the garage door was closed. My heart was beating rapidly with excitement at the thought of the gift I was about to bestow on him, one that would be given with love.

It all happened so fast, I opened the door and barely stepped out and he was in my face and not pleased to see me. This soft-spoken southern gentleman had pressed his body against mine and said "This is not a good time ... Mary." There was coldness in his voice. "I have someone here ... and you've been drinking, let me take you home." "No, I'm not drunk!" I insisted. "And I don't want to go home! I'm okay with this! That's what I've come to tell you." Then everything became ugly as the sharp swords of our tongues battled, and the words became colder and harsher. Who would win?

Paul grabbed my arms as I walked toward the house and his grip took me back to another time, a time I gave up the fight, and I was no longer standing here and now but at home, in mother's living room, and the grip that held me down so tightly was not Paul's. It was my attacker's! This time I fought, punching him in his chest and screaming, "I hate you! I hate you!" The more Paul tightened his grip, the harder I punched him and the louder I screamed those words over and over. This deep-rooted rage that was hidden in the dark chambers of my mind rose to protect me. This time I was not giving up, he was not going to overpower me. I got free and ran toward the front door, then as I turned to see Paul, my mind flashed back and everything was a blur. I could hear someone yelling, "Dial 911." No, I never saw *who* was there.

Those hands were on me again and I pushed them away in a panic and managed to open the front door and run through; I was running for my life. I did it, I was free! Visions of emerald green foliage and tall whispering evergreens were sucked away through a vacuum of lifeless walls of plaster. Where was I? Who had control of the remote, fast forward, then replay? I had just run away from my attacker, out the front door at home.......I know I did, I was just standing in my front yard. How can I be here standing in Paul's living room? Now he and I are yelling and running through the kitchen, I knocked that vase of flowers over on the table and locked myself in the bathroom. He was yelling at me through the door, "Mary, the police are here, you're going to be arrested, do you hear me?" I remember saying, "You can't do that, I'll lose my job." And then thinking, "My name will be in the papers, how will I explain this to my sons?"

Okay, I have to come out of the bathroom but I'm not looking forward to seeing the police out there. I could feel the tears about to flow, holding them back and with a quick turn of my wrist the door was open and I was on the run again. Running up the stairs to the second floor or was I running down the street on the hard black pavement? Trying to focus my eyes and clear my head, he is here.......I can feel his breath on the back of my neck and a chill has entered my body. My eyes do not see him and my thoughts are only of getting away.   Pain was in my chest from the rapid pounding of my heart as it too raced to escape.   There I was watching myself from the bubble floating above, running in and out of rooms but, when I stepped back into the hall, the rooms were gone. And I was running past pine trees through the snow-covered woods and the fear did not freeze my steps as it had in the past.   As I ran out of the woods and down the hill, one step at a time until my feet hit the bottom of the landing of the staircase and, where was the hill?   Who was I running to find, the person who called "911"?   Who was I running from – my attacker?

Anger and fear gave way to control and clarity, and I was no longer angry.   The fear was left behind, never to step past the landing of those stairs.   In today's world of domestic violence, if a "911" call is made to the police, they must respond and the normal procedure is that someone must be arrested. In the kitchen as I was confronted by the police, Paul did not want to press charges and I was allowed to make a call to obtain a ride home.   Both he and I had been drinking and given the events that just transpired, the police thought I had way too much alcohol to be responsible for driving.   That was not the case, but no one that night would ever know the true events that had occurred.

It's funny how life plays out.   I remember saying to my ex-husband on many occasions "It all works out the way God has planned, everything has a reason," although he disagreed. He would often say after the divorce, "Call me, Mary, if you ever need anything."   And in the same breath he'd say, "I know you won't … will you?"   Well, I never had before, but tonight changed all that and he got his wish.

There were two police officers on the scene ready to uphold the law, but it must have been apparent that no crime had been committed, all the signs were of a lovers' quarrel, a situation out of control but not dangerous. Don't ask me to identify them in a line-up, as the only thing I would be able to identify was Paul's eyes. As I was being escorted through the house out the front door by these two men in blue, the last thing I remember of that night was staring at Paul standing in the front yard and the look in his eyes. Is this the way we would say our good-byes? There was sadness in my heart and compassion in my eyes, but the words "I love you" were never spoken. I walked straight across the yard in slow motion toward the police cruiser and Paul walked toward the left side yard heading to the back of the house. Our bodies were moving in one direction but our heads were turned by the magnetic emotions our eyes communicated, and with one last step he was gone out of sight and I stepped into the cruiser.

From this point on, it was voices heard from afar, the police officer asking questions and someone responding. I just stared out the window and suddenly we were there parked next to my ex's car. I don't recall what was said, their mouths were moving ... like a silent movie, but where were the subtitles? Emotionless I got out of the cruiser and got into his car. The only words I heard were, "Mary, what did you do?" He took me to his house and poured us a drink, Jim Beam, his favorite bourbon, then gave me a tour. It was all a silent movie and I could not tell now if I was a player or a member of the audience. If I spoke, I didn't hear my words and his mouth was moving but there were no sounds. This man I was married to for twenty-eight years had no clue. Did he not see this zombie who walked two steps behind as he flaunted the changes he had made to the house that once was ours? The feeling of being in this bubble; that's all I remember, then morning came.

He drove me to the location where I was to meet the police and they drove me to Paul's house to get my car. It was early morning, and I wondered if Paul was inside watching, as I scraped the snow from my front windows. There was white everywhere, white snow, virgin snow, and the morning sun rising in the sky sent rays of light through the trees, and I could hear the sound of birds singing. This new day had set everything right again and all was peaceful to the … On Looker! No time to waste as I was being watched by someone, and it was the police, making sure I left with no disturbance. So, quickly I got into my car and drove away, but this time I was in control.

Dream

One night after this event, I had a dream. It seemed so real to me, as though it just happened, so I jumped out of bed and ran to the window to see. Where was he? So, I sat at my desk and wrote this poem to describe my dream.

He Says Good-Bye

I close my eyes and go to sleep
The darkness shadows over me
Through blinking eyes I see the light
Then he is clearly out of sight

The floor boards squeak one by one
The shallow man is finally gone
Then down the stairs and through the door
He runs and screams, I love no more

With broken heart I flee my bed
In hopes to catch a glimpse of him
Down the stairs my feet take me
Just in time to see him leave

I scream, I yell, "Don't leave me!"
But all he does is laugh and tease
He laughs and laughs until I cry
Then finally he says, "Good-Bye."

Then I began to write another poem, to describe the loss of my love. My memories took me back to the beginning, before the demons roamed, and the slithering worm for which he sought.

A Love Lost

I close my eyes then open wide
To see your smile and what's inside
With captive eyes you dazzle me
My love runs wild and so you see

In candle light you still pursue
Of what you see and what you knew
Is it love or is it lust
Can it be that I must trust?

These worry dreams that steal the night
And always say that you are right
Right to love and right to lust
Forbidden fruit I must not touch

Drink from your lips sweet as wine
Then smother me or say you're mine
Can it be that you are wrong
I am right it feels so strong

Hearts that beat with pounding thunder
That you may lie and I may wonder
And passion flows throughout the night
Is it wrong or is it right

Fires burn deep inside
Ashes flicker when alive
We love no more, you cry and shout
It must be lust without a doubt

Then you say in your dreams it's only she
That sets a fire inside of me
Forgive me, Dear, for I have lied
You could not know what was inside

This shallow man I have become
To love and lie and leave someone
Can't you see that I am wrong
I should not love for I'm not strong

In my heart you'll always be
For the love you once gave me
Love so true that I shattered
Forgive me, Dear, that's all that matters

It Was Lillie

They say go home and sleep on it – everything looks better in the morning; well, not this time. The morning sun brought reality, reality of what I had done and by this I was traumatized. I needed desperately to talk to someone, but not just anyone; it had to be someone who would not judge me, someone I could trust to give me the right advice and someone who really cared. I called someone I had never met and she consoled me; we spoke at length, it seemed for hours, and she did not judge me. She was understanding and compassionate and her voice was soothing; through the phone lines from the state of Maryland she sent me love and I embraced every word.

We spoke daily for the first week and each call would begin in the same manner – "Hi, Lillie. It's Mary." I wondered if she knew the power her words held, as I shared with her the grim details of that last night at Paul's house and my saga of the rape. Through her interpretations my reactions to the events began to make more sense. She thought because I had focused on Paul's face during the rape that I was confusing him with the attacker. At the end of each call exhaustion would take over from all the tears cried. This forty-seven-year-old, soft-spoken southern lady was Paul's older sister. We had never met but I had seen photos. She was fair in complexion, had dark blonde hair, a wonderfully kind face, the brightest smile and the sincerest blue eyes. We had been writing letters and calling to chat over the past few years and a real bond had been woven; we were friends, friends for always.

No wonder Lillie was so calm when we spoke; this was not the first time she had heard my story. Paul had called her earlier, and in her words, "Paul didn't realize how sick you really are!" She was referring to the aftermath of the rape and that last night at his house. Lillie said, "I told Paul to stay away for your sake, he's not helping you, Mary. I can't guarantee he'll listen but you shouldn't have any more contact." She just kept insisting that the only person of importance was me, that I needed to take care of myself and in her words, "No one else should matter."

I knew she was right. I didn't want to be sick ... it hurt so much ... those words, "Paul didn't realize how sick you really are!" Was he afraid of me? Does she think he should be? Even in my hour of need, my thoughts were on the chaos of others and my need to set things right. But as Lillie said, "Paul is a big guy and he will deal with it." Taking her advice, I let it go, placed it in God's hands and moved forward. Lillie had guided me in the right direction and soon every Saturday morning was spent talking to a counselor from the Rape Crisis Center in a nearby town. Then my weekly chat with Lillie would follow.

Distorted interpretations of those events and a sort of anger generated from Ms. Zest in our next session. "Do you know the danger you placed yourself in? If the officer had handcuffed you and you fought with him – he would not have known what you were going though. You could have been hurt if you had flipped out on them." There was a sense of panic for my safety, real concern in her voice. Then she proceeded to say, "Mary, you can't go on like that, people don't know what's going on in your mind, they don't know what you've been through. Promise me you won't attempt anything like that again. Promise me." At those words the image of being handcuffed and the feelings of panic come, as I see myself fighting with the officer, being wrestled to the ground and under the full moon, insanity takes hold. She and I discuss this thought and the reality that could have been. How could I survive being locked up in an institution?

My sessions with Ms. Zest were becoming more infrequent; as I became stronger, we said our good-byes, never to have another session. After a couple of months of counseling from the Rape Crisis Center, I was on my own, left with only my art as a cushion. This cushion is a wonderful thing … you can carry it with you in the car, on the beach and even sneak it into work.

There was a cushion of another kind that caressed me at night as I slipped it over my head, tugging on the tails of that very worn T-shirt as it hugged my hips. The caress was felt all the way down to my knees. Each night I would climb into bed, roll over onto my right side and pull the collar up over my nose. Some people spray fragrances such as lavender on their bed pillows to induce calmness and sleep. But, for me, one deep inhale and the scent embedded in the fibers of that special shirt were all I needed for a good night's sleep.

Then one night the scent disappeared and the calmness turned to sadness. Mistakenly I had tossed this shirt into the wash; no, not the wash! Bellows could be heard as I cried out … how could this happen? The sadness was now mourning, mourning for the death of a scent, the scent of Paul. As sad as this was, it was an accident that was meant to be – another means of letting go. So as with all deaths, the burial followed and this worn, white ordinary shirt was laid to rest in a plastic bag and tossed into the trash. And with this burial I gained strength to move on.

Looking back in my art journal, I see that one of the last works I did was that of a Rooster. Sitting in my living room at my desk, I glanced over at the left-over stamp – it was a small square with a black rooster standing sideways in the middle on a background of bright blue. The yellow morning sun had risen behind its head, which was cast in red. This stamp I had placed in the middle of this eight-by-eleven sheet of paper and then, with yellow and green pastels, I drew sun rays all around the outside edges of the stamp. In the bottom right corner in pink I drew a heart. I remember that the students in my class just looked at this art with no expression – they must have thought, "What is this?"

On the back of the page I wrote these words:

> I looked up and God had planted a vision of a new day in my mind. Every day is a new life and as I looked up, the Rooster stamp was drawing my hands and heart to caress it, and my new life was to begin. My classical music had set the tone for joyous celebrations; what once was ugly and painful does not feel so deeply implanted in my soul. I have learned how to live, love and smile in Satan's Garden of Thorns.

> Thank you for allowing me to feel sadness.
> "I have found my heart!"

Triggers

Females are so intuitive and Natasha, in her soft-spoken manner, almost caught me in a vulnerable moment of weakness. We have shared many deep emotions and secrets, but not this one and as trusting in her as I was, the fact that she was a co-worker would not allow this secret to be shared. The fear of being exposed outweighed my trust in her secrecy, or maybe it was just a sure doubt in my own judgment – nonetheless, my words were silent.

Testing the waters – In April 2002, Natasha and I had attended an annual reunion held at a restaurant in Connecticut. These were Natasha's co-workers from a former employer and a very close-knit group. Knowing I would be uncomfortable but wanting to test unfamiliar waters, I decided to focus on pleasant thoughts and leave my fear in the parking lot. As I walked through the crowded room, glancing towards the bar, then at the many tables, searching for Natasha, the sensation of someone's breath blowing against my neck sent chills down my spine, then my arms flew to strike out as I quickly turned to defend myself. There I was, standing in the middle of the room, oh … what a sight!

Did anyone see me combatting the air? A bit embarrassed I sat at the first vacant table and waited for Natasha to arrive. Head held high, I waited for what seemed an eternity but in fact was ten minutes, for this blonde-haired beauty to arrive. As she walked across the floor toward my table, heads turned and as she approached the table, so did a flow of men. Not only is she young and beautiful, the magnet of her personality draws attention wherever she might grace with her presence.

After the introductions, and a couple of cocktails and conversation, we all dispersed into the backroom where the buffet was set up and posters of photos taken at past reunions were arranged around the room. Standing away from the buffet line in a close circle, deep in conversation, were Natasha and four of her male friends; standing within the circle, in her own conversation with fear, was me. Fear left outside in the parking lot crept into this circle of friends.

Transforming this fear into a comforting face, I had focused myself on thoughts of Paul – this worked; fear surrendered as I felt his body press up against my back, then his hands slid around my waist to the front of my belly, as I rested my hands on his. This was a perfect fit and as my head tilted slightly, his lips lightly kissed my cheek. Glancing up into his eyes, I let out a scream. I had been daydreaming and this man, a co-worker and friend of Natasha, had mistaken me for someone else. He was just as shocked as I was when our eyes met. He apologized for startling me but confessed he had enjoyed the caress.

Everyone laughed and, to those on the outside it may have appeared as a comedy, but from my view it was a tragedy, and I needed to run away. From the moment our eyes met the fight or flight of panic could not be shaken.

Pulling Natasha off to one side and telling her I was ill allowed for my escape.

***

In June 2002, I was on disability leave for carpal tunnel of my left wrist, but the pain had heightened as the sensation of needles stabbing under the flesh increased in magnitude, unbearable, and surgery was inevitable. I was unaware the past would resurface. On arrival at the Westerly Hospital, I performed all the normal formalities--checking in, completing insurance forms, and signing permission forms. Then I was escorted to the preoperative ward to change into the johnny gown for surgery.

The staff took no chances for errors; every member of that operative team interviewed me. One by one, doctor, nurse, anesthesiologist and a few others entered the holding room to record my answers to their identical questions. Does anyone know who's doing what? Later I was told this process was established to eliminate errors – you know the headlines, "Lady To Have Tummy Tuck Receives Breast Implant In Error."

As I lay on the surgical bed, the attendant rolled the bed into the hall and left me alone. Chills set in and my hands became clammy, no panties! Oh, no, I have no panties on and someone might see ... down there. The thought of being touched when sedated frightened me. What if they touch me in places other than my arm? What if they take this gown off and expose my vaginal area? What if they do something to me ... I won't know!

Many scenarios rushed into the foreground, exacerbating my worst fears. The anesthesiologist approached to comfort the normal patient's fear of surgery ... I was not

94

the normal patient and this he would realize soon. Meanwhile, as we spoke I exhibited only confidence and composure and as I agreed without hesitation to the method of sedation, he pushed the bed down the hall into the operating room.

Laughter emanates from the sterile walls as the staff prepares. Eyes wide, scanning the room, and slipping further back in time I ask to be covered, "Please cover me with a blanket." One sweet-smiling nurse leans over to explain, "I am going to strap a device around your thigh; this will act as a ground." "I don't have panties on, please don't let anyone see me, please keep me covered."

Repeating these words over and over again and the impulse to cover, to protect, increased as I pulled at the gown, tucking it securely under my legs. Then tilting my head to the left, was I visible? Are all doctors so emotionless? He was focusing on his task at hand – my hand, then strapping it securely to this extension; it was almost curtain time. Let the show begin!

Instructions are echoed from the left, right, at my head, from the foot area. The volume turned up and screams, then more screams perpetuating, movement restricted. "Cover me, don't let anyone see me. Don't tie me down! Don't tie me down!" Screaming and crying, "I'm not afraid of the surgery...it's not that. Really it's not that. Please don't hurt me." Fighting the restraints, thrashing my head back and forth and hysterically screaming, "It's not you, it's not you, it's something that happened to me." That sweet smiling nurse leaned over, stroking my head, attempting to calm my shaking body, as she repeated, "Tell me what it is, what happened? Talk to me." The anesthesia was taking effect. Reliving the rape, the terror, I am fighting to regain control of here and now before sedation overcomes my being. Fighting to speak the words, "It's not your fault, it's nothing you did." Desperately needing to explain my actions, but how could I? To truly explain meant humiliation; haven't I humiliated myself enough? There is rapid breathing, then exhaustion, and in a flicker, the candle is blown out.

***

Where Did the Nightmares Go

It is September 2002 and I have moved into my new home. A two-story colonial, cream in color, sage green (these colors of past life welcome me home) shutters and front door, with a one-car garage. My new beginning! The neighborhood is an older established one, with some retirees, some young families and a couple of us divorcees. I felt right at home even before I had moved in. Within minutes the sandy beach can be cushioning my feet because it's just a two-mile drive or a wonderful walk on a sunny day to my favorite place, the beach.

In a cardboard box found on the top shelf of my walk-in bedroom closet are the many cards Lillie had sent as words of encouragement – they are treasures – the threads which sometimes held me together in the early days of my recovery. And as a reminder of those days, mounted in an emerald green and gold marbled frame hanging on the kitchen wall is one of those cards.

On faded white paper with the texture of fibers are splashes of color. These very primitive flowers sparkle with glitter, and shades of lavender, mauve and yellow, as warm wishes dance across the page.

Wishing you …
Time
to enjoy the gift of each day.
Laughter
to help meet life's many challenges.
Friends
to share your joy.
Dreams
to keep you going.

Little does she know how much her kindness is gracing my home. This is a remembrance of how far I've come. Sitting in the middle of my bedroom on the cold wooden floor unpacking the many boxes, I found the teddy bear Lillie had sent. Her name is 'Mary' and she is tattooed. Yes, on the bottom of her left foot are stitched the letters M-A-R-Y. When I was a child sleeping with a teddy bear helped me to feel safe from all the boogie-men that roamed at night. Now sleeping with a teddy bear, rubbing this coarse brown fur against my face is soothing – there are no boogie-men to be found.

The strangest thing happened when I moved into my house; the nightmares stopped. Demons and nightmares were left behind. I was so relaxed, not afraid and at the end of each day, sleep would take hold of me and I could sleep for hours. This was my safe haven – nothing or no one could enter and harm me here. Like that virgin canvas, this newly constructed home was not stained with memories and the aura generating from within is mine alone.

Every home should have a puppy and that was a means of discussion between mother and me. She was dead set against me having a dog of any kind. But it was my home and my life, so off I went to the Animal Rescue League in hopes of saving the life of a puppy, a beagle. No puppy, the only beagle was a five-year-old, over-weight, unresponsive dog. A playful puppy was what I had set out to find; this was a disappointment and a waste of my gas and time, an hour and thirty minute drive for this!

The attendant placed a leash around her neck and said, "We've named her Maggie." Well, I'm here – let's take her for a walk out to the fenced-in courtyard. Once there; the leash was removed so she could run. "Maaa-ggie, Maaa-ggie," singing out her name, "Come here, girl." Didn't appear she recognized her own name, could it be she's deaf? Definitely overweight, her belly almost touched the ground as she waddled across the courtyard; I placed the leash back around her neck and returned her to the attendant.

Walking toward my car, I turned to say good-bye and Maggie looked so sad, the many folds in her face gave her the appearance of depression. Three months housed here and she is on borrowed time, her days are numbered. If I won't take her, who will? That day a life was saved. She was distrustful of everyone who came into her path, hunkering down in a frozen position every time anyone attempted to stroke her head. Sudden movements sent her into fright. On a routine phone call from the Animal Rescue League inquiring on our progress, I was told she had been abused. "She is a keeper." It was meant to be and in time she learned to trust and like her mistress, but even this trust was guarded.

As months passed, wonderful memories have been painted within the walls of this haven, Christmas parties, Mardi Gras parties, family gatherings, and so on. A mixture of married friends, as well as my single ladies, have been entertained here and they all look forward to the annual events. Not wanting to stain these memories, I have never invited a *single* male friend into my home. Ties have been severed from all eligible males and unlike the old Mary, I do not have male friends.

Binging has become - a favorite pastime. Eat, eat and eat! Every night down a half-gallon of deep dark chocolate ice cream, the extra rich chocolate with chocolate pieces and nuts. Yum, yum, good! Why cook? Tear open a bag of chips and pour your bourbon over ice and there's supper. Who says you can't make a meal out of fast foods? This was my way of hiding. Hiding from men. Getting them not to notice me.

Soon this healthy, fit, mature lady was unfit, but jolly and within six months had blossomed thirty pounds heavier. It's funny, the same old me but heavier and men pass right by, no second glances or turn of the heads. Sweat shirts and sweat pants cover a large territory and there is room to grow … my comfort zone. Ten more pounds and now I'm up to one hundred and seventy-eight pounds. You might have thought I was walking through life with blinders on.

Tucked away in this comfort zone, under these excess pounds, was a very discontented, lonely woman, drifting into solitude and detaching myself from all emotions. My spirit is wilting, the glowing flame within is but a soft flicker and without oxygen this flame will smother.

Gone are the days of walks on the beach alone. There is so much I miss of the old Mary. It took a few trips to the beach and the inability to walk more than forty feet before I realized what was holding me back -- *FEAR.* For years I've walked alone on the beaches at Misquamicut, the off-season is my favorite time. The tourists have left, and with the exception of a few locals – the beach is mine. What is wrong?

After driving two miles to get here, I park the car close to the walkway entrance then start out to enjoy the sounds of the ocean, and carrying my backpack full of snacks, towel and radio, I walk onto the beach. Usually I carry my sneakers with laces tied together, flung over my shoulder. Toes pressing with massaging motion through the grains of sand, I take one step, then two steps, with sneakers flopping to this beat of my footsteps.

Once at the edge of the water, I plant my feet firmly into the sand and wait. The foaming waves roll into shore with such power that it scoops trenches around my feet and as the tide rushes back out to sea, like soldiers, my feet hold their ground then I am left standing on two small islands. Childish behaviors, splashing each step, as I walk down the beach alone on the shoreline. Sometimes the fog rolls in and before I can turn myself around to head back, dampness covers my hair and penetrates my clothes. It is easy to visualize pirates in the distant fog, maybe Captain Hook's pirate ship. At the end of these walks I am definitely destressed. I miss those walks, I miss the old Mary.

It hits you, the image in the mirror and the question, "Who is that lady? What have I done to myself? That's not me looking back at me." I was on that seesaw, one moment up, next moment down. Depression was attempting to breach the walls of my sane world but I was not going to allow the invasion. Hurdles in life are meant to be overcome. Realizing what I have done to myself, I know a weight loss plan must be followed, so I start the program and toss the sweats to the back of my closet. Lose the comfort! As the weight starts to drop, more interest in cosmetics and clothing takes over and the old Mary is being revitalized.

A void gradually creeps into my heart; I miss the touch of a man, the smell of his flesh and the companionship that only a man can give a woman. How do I meet a man? My friends don't know any eligible men, and I don't hang out at bars and dating men from work is not a wise habit to start.

Eventually the story of the rape would have to come up and my co-workers would find out. So, I decided to join a dating service on the Internet; some of my friends are doing the same thing and they are dating. Was I ready? Can I trust? How will I react? So many questions ran through my mind. But, in the end I knew that, to continue this healing process and to enjoy a full life, chances must be taken. I had to step outside this haven and explore the world again.

I remember a gift I gave to Lillie one year – it was a book of wishes and I had placed a bookmark in one page, this wish I had for her. On the left page was pictured a young girl, maybe age ten, standing in front of her birthday cake, which was lit with candles, and she was about to make her wish and blow them out. Down the right page was all the wishes a friend would have for her and the last wish was, "Don't forget to dance," meaning the dance of life.

Today I want this wish for me. I want to Dance with Life! In time, I have met many nice men through this dating service but am not able to feel comfortable in this close environment. I cringe each time one of these men touches my hands, or places his arm around my shoulder and I try not to pull away. With great effort I have allowed myself to be kissed, but when the date is over, I can't wait to get home to rinse my mouth out and wash my hands or take a shower and get his smell off my skin. Eventually after several months I discontinued the membership and I have fallen back into my old routines. I like to think of it as, I have just taken a break, not given up!

Ryan

Last week after the snowstorm my dear friend Dotty and I met for lunch at this cozy little restaurant in Narragansett called Crazy Burgers. It is located on a residential street with the seating capacity of about thirty, so we were lucky to be seated. The interior is decorated in a combination of 'Hippie 60's' and Oriental with an artsy flare. The menu is a bit crazy, but with palate-pleasing delights for the adventurous patrons. We shared a phyllo pastry sandwich filled with salmon salad smothered in a secret sauce and then we washed it down with hot cider. In the midst of all this sharing were conversations and the topic of Ryan.

In early January of 2003, I had met this thirty-eight-year-old Lebanese man one night at a restaurant – we both were sitting at the bar watching the football game on TV. He turned to me and asked which team I was rooting for and, embarrassed, I admitted ignorance of the game … not understanding anything about football. As our conversation continued, and the game finished with the New England Patriots winning, Ryan asked if I was married or dating anyone and when my reply was "No," he asked if I would like to go out to dinner sometime. I was distrustful, over analyzing every word spoken as he enlightened me with his story of divorce and family heritage. Ryan is but three years older than my eldest son -- do I dare? I had intended to have only one cold beer then leave for home but found myself sipping on a second drink, compliments of Ryan.

I must admit the attention felt rather good and what does age mean anyway? Men do it all the time, date younger women. It's the trend today, younger men are interested in older women and this just might be the experience I need. After all he did make me laugh, I didn't feel threatened, just a bit nervous. We walked out to the parking lot together and maybe because the parking lot was well lit, I was not afraid. "Well, Ryan ... if you give me your phone number, I'll call you sometime but I don't usually give out my number." Before these words completely rolled from my mouth he had jotted his cell phone number down on a piece of paper. "You're not going to call, are you?" Ryan thought I wouldn't call and I thought he was right. But, after tossing around all the pros and cons for a couple of days, the pros won out and I made the call, to his surprise, and mine!

Ryan and I met a couple of times just for drinks and sandwiches and to play a game of pool. Dotty asked, "What don't you like about him?" "Well, he smokes and slips with the *F* word on occasion and goes overboard with the compliments." Then I thought he's just horny and implies romantic endeavors and as much as these characteristics were not appealing to me, I was getting that tingling feeling in areas of my body that I thought were dead and that sure felt good. We're not really dating and I'm already worried about the next step... about sex. Do I want to have sex? Yes. Right now I just want to know that I could enjoy this act without flipping out, without going crazy.

But then again, to have sex for the sake of just having sex with no emotional attachment – could I do that? Could I do that without seeing Paul's face? Could I do that without seeing Tony's face? And as Dotty explains, "You're the only one who can give you permission. You do know that, and I'm not judging you – who am I to judge? They say people who live in glass houses shouldn't throw stones and I think everything happens for a reason and if it feels right, then, Mary… go for it!"

As we talked the subject changed many times, and one conversation we had was about the latest sexual experiences young people are experimenting with these days. It's all over the talk shows – teens from the age of twelve-years and up playing this new game: Spin the bottle for oral sex. Can you imagine your twelve-year-old daughter engaged in the act of oral sex while her friends stand by watching and waiting and maybe cheering her on? According to the shows, teens today don't consider oral sex as real sex. "Dotty, here I am fifty-three years old and feeling guilty just contemplating intercourse. How silly is that?" Well, when we departed that afternoon, I left Dotty with a different view of me and I took away a different viewpoint from her.

It's been two weeks since Dotty and I shared that sandwich and I've enjoyed a couple more dates with Ryan. Yes, finally after so many agonizing hours of analyzing my viewpoints and attacking the question of my engaging in a deliberate act of sex with a near stranger, someone that I was not in love with but was attracted to sexually, I had decided to commit myself to this affair.

It's February 4th, and the night Ryan invited me to his home for the first time. After our dinner date I followed him to his house. As I walked across this very long narrow porch to the front door, the night air was crisp, stars illuminated the sky and my thoughts flashed back to my conversation with Dotty and her words, "If it feels right, go for it." I had reservations but for the most part, my thoughts were that it was right for me. I need to know if I can feel sensual again. I need to know that I can trust another man with my body and I sense that he will be gentle with me. Can I trust these instincts?

Ryan's warm hand slipped from my grip and he pulled me close and smiled, "I just want to show you my house. We can have a cocktail if you like and finish the evening relaxing in the hot tub." He seemed very relaxed already and I wondered how many cocktails Ryan had indulged in before our dinner date. As I walked through the threshold my dead flesh awakened and I was consumed with sexual desires and I, too, was very relaxed, as the dinner cocktails had tranquilized me.

Okay Mary, you're a big girl – don't fret, just let it all go and enjoy the moment, it's not a commitment. The hardest thing for me was to stop thinking about the what-ifs, what would people think? Crap, it's all crap; you can do this, who's going to know? Empty your head of all that stuff and focus on yourself and pleasure. If Ryan could hear this stupid conversation I was engaged in, he might think I was a vulnerable child that he could take advantage of and manipulate. As I stared up into his soft mocha brown eyes and reached out to caress his face, words didn't need to be spoken; just the glow from my face alone was his answer.

Ryan broke his left leg and ankle three months back and has not returned to work, still recovering from the surgery and the implant of a few metal rods to hold his leg together. He walks with a slight limp, favoring his bad leg, an outward sign of vulnerability. As I followed Ryan's footsteps through the open floor plan of his house and up the center staircase to the second floor on this one-man guided tour, my whole body tingled with excitement, as my desires grew stronger, but my heart did not throb with love. It was as if the dead in me was given a reprieve and I was alive again.

This limp of favoritism was a reminder of desires past. Paul, too, had a distinctive gimp in his walk, but my desire with him was of love. Tonight my thoughts and emotions must be focused as there was an agenda ahead and the return trip down those hardwood stairs would only take place once my agenda was accomplished. Ryan's talking away in this slight accent, giving origin of his many purchases of furnishings and which items his ex-wife would be taking to her apartment. "Mary, this spare bedroom set is going but look here; this is the master bedroom and this is my bed ... I'm keeping it. Isn't it big? And look here in my bathroom, the hot tub." What did I hear? Was that a quiver in his voice as he asked, "Should I draw the water?" "Why, Ryan, are you nervous, too?" With this the sound of water splashing echoed into the bedroom and sitting on this California-size bed, I watched Ryan drop his clothes to the floor. The heat from his hard young body escaped into the air just as his clothes made contact with the floor and like a humid summer evening's breeze, it look my breath away. My mouth began to water and my hands turned cold. Ryan looked down at me with eyes of desire and smiled with a grin of satisfaction and he kissed me. "Ryan," I said, "Go ahead, I'll be right in."

What will happen when I walk through that doorway toward the hot tub stark naked? What will I see in Ryan's eyes, disappointment? He must have felt the flab around my waist when he held me in his arms. My body was that of a mature nature, soft and comfortable. Well, my agenda wasn't to look wonderful – it was to have a sexual experience and not freak out, to pass the test I had just placed before me. It didn't feel wrong; on the contrary, it felt extremely right to be here and now with Ryan. I wasn't the only one with an agenda ...

it was quite evident for the past few dates that Ryan wanted to entertain his desires, too.

Standing so vulnerable in the middle of this room, my clothes, too, fell to the floor; then finding composure, breathe in, hold tummy in; okay, walk towards the doorway with confidence, everything will be okay. With each step my toes curled, grabbing the pile of soft carpet as a stabilizer and thoughts of retreating caused my footsteps to pause. The room was romantic with candles casting flickers of light up the walls and it seemed as though these flickers danced across Ryan's olive-colored skin like fireflies and the scent of his cologne tantalized my senses. The cool tile floor beneath my feet drew heat from my body as I walked with eyes fixed on Ryan's smile – that wonderful smile that made me feel comfortable with myself and this soft mature body.

"You're beautiful." Those were his words. It didn't matter if he truly meant them; just the mere fact that they were spoken was enough.

The memory of that evening fades and then refocuses and the words, "Mary, it's Ryan. Are you okay? No one's going to hurt you. Calm down … it's okay, it's Ryan." Ryan's words repeated over and over again. My body was stiff and my fists were gripped so tight that fingernail marks were etched into the palms of my hands. I could hear his soft voice reassuring me that everything was okay and he was with me.

Opening my eyes I saw Ryan's face and felt his hands stroking my hair back. I don't know how long I was in that other place and I don't remember us leaving the hot tub and climbing into bed and does it matter? - Not really. I was not afraid. Ryan brought me back to reality and even though I had slipped away to that other place and my body reacted with these distorted movements, there were no visions, no visions of Tony, no visions of Paul, no visions of the rape. But my body had reacted with pain, pain with internal contact. Those gates had been locked and I had lost the key to open them. Tears flowed down my cheeks as I confessed my secret to Ryan and he listened with compassion and understanding. This was my true confession of my secretive agenda for the night – to use him, to use his body to conquer and recover completely myself.

I did not elaborate on details of the rape, only the fact that I had been raped. Ryan's words came hesitantly and a bit harsh, "Stop, stop, don't say anymore, it's okay. That bastard, how could anyone do that? How long ago was it, recently? Do you know who he was? What do you want, his legs broken? I know people in New York … just let me know. I can take care of him for you." His strong emotions surprised me and I was comfortable looking into his eyes; there was no shame, I had not done anything wrong, it was not my fault. Ryan will never know how much he helped me that night and I was right to trust my instincts, he is a good man. Ryan held me tenderly in his arms, tucking the comforter up around my neck; he whispered in my ear, "You can use me anytime, baby," and I drifted off to sleep feeling so very safe and understood.

In the morning that lost key was found and under sober conditions, the gates were open and the woman in me was restored. Driving home that morning, I thought of Ms. Zest and our many sessions – would she approve of my tactics, the extent I've gone to, to test myself, to gain answers, to have closure? In hindsight maybe it was reckless, maybe I was rushing my recovery, wanting to jump ahead to know I was okay. And even though the gates were open, the water from the fountain never flowed and that was okay for me because I passed the test. And who deserves the credit? Ryan, for making me feel so comfortable, or me, for staying focused and allowing myself to be vulnerable? At any rate I've learned more about who I am, the Mary inside, under all that soft comfortable flesh, a woman who needs passion and a strong loving commitment to make love with a man. The experience left behind with Ryan was not one of love, passion, attachment, or affection; I experienced no emotions and without these the fountain would not flow.

Painful Memories and
Doing Stupid Stuff

Coping with the residue left behind as a survivor of rape wasn't easy and some of the stupid things I've done almost caused me the loss of family and friends. Why? Because I did not share the experience with them and they were not able to rationalize what my behavior was all about. I was addicted to alcohol, drinking every day, carrying travel mugs filled with bourbon, drinking and driving; I was an accident about to happen.

One Friday evening in October 2001, Paul arrived home to find me passed out in my car and all doors were locked. I would never know the panic he was in; attempting to rescue me from myself. When I was finally coherent enough to speak it was morning; I was curled up in bed; my head pounding like a jackhammer. Paul deserved to be angry; however, he never showed anger. But when I asked questions of that night, "How did you get me out of the car? Did I throw up all over the place? How much of a mess did I make? Did you clean me up?" His only comments were, "You don't want to know. Forget it! Let's not talk about it! Let's just move on." The stench of vomit permeated the air and lingered on my palette, lying in bed, room spinning and hating this person

I've become and upset with Paul for not being home when I arrived.

If he had been home I wouldn't have had to struggle with the key, this stupid key that did not work and I couldn't get the door open. Now waiting in the car, crackling noises echoed through the pine trees – locking the doors just in case. Well, he'll be coming soon or so I thought, but as time passed, flashbacks emerged; with every crackling noise my breath paused and my body cringed. I could not calm myself down, I just knew there was someone out there.

October is the month to celebrate Halloween and of course, we were going to a party on Saturday night; so, there was a bottle of bourbon in my car. This was our drink for the party. Just a couple of swigs, just one or two, that's all I'll drink right from the bottle, this should help me to relax until Paul gets home. No one is out there. No one is going to get me. Sights and sounds of the rape won't leave me. I turn the radio on in hope of drowning out these sounds in my head, his voice, his words, "He's only with you for the sex." More swigs of bourbon from the bottle, I swallow and swallow more until the only sound is that of the glass bottle tapping against my front teeth as I swallow. As my body relaxes, the images fade and the crackling noises are just crackling noises. Like the images I, too, slowly faded away, leaving behind only a few swigs in the quart bottle of bourbon.

***

There was a surprise birthday party in June 2003 for my daughter-in-law and it was *not* my pleasure to disrupt and destroy this precious event. Bill had worked very hard planning the party, cooking wonderful foods, decorating the works. His wife is close with her cousins, aunts and uncles and there were probably thirty relatives, including small children, on that day to celebrate this special occasion. Then there was my ex-husband and his friend, my mother, my son Rob and his family. Everyone was having a great time out on the deck, music playing and I was sitting at the picnic table talking to one of the cousins and sipping my third glass of Merlot.

Staring at my ex-husband across the deck, I saw him laughing in conversation with the boys. My thoughts drifted back to Paul and my inability to respond to intimacy, reliving the rape. I was drowning in pity, feeling inadequate and desperately wanting to feel whole again. Drinking too much, trying to cope, wanting a solution now. Maybe it would be different if I had sex with my ex-husband? "Mary, where are these thoughts coming from?"

Questioning myself, but thinking that maybe it might work. Merlot, the third glass combined with my confused state of mind was a disastrous combination. Across the deck I walked, not very steadily, heading straight for him. The only thing I remember is that I was flirting with him. The next morning I woke up on Bill's sofa. Apparently I had made a scene and passed out, embarrassed myself and disrupted the party. Well, no apology could erase the image etched in the cool air that lingered into the morning.

A couple of days later Bill's wife called me to discuss her concerns that I might have a drinking problem, but there was no way my true intent was going to be revealed, so I listened. I listened to her valid concerns, knowing I was at fault. The relationship she and I had was already strained, in my perspective it was virtually nonexistent – this was not the relationship I wanted.

Not being blessed with a daughter, as my first child a girl, died in my womb in the eighth month of pregnancy, the special bond between a mother and her daughter was not meant for me, and the emptiness felt far after delivery could never be filled.

***

The loss of a child under any circumstance is horrific and some families never survive. Some families pull forces together and become stronger while others are torn and fall apart. Divorce becomes the result; unlike the relationship between my spouse and me, as we were held in limbo before, and after, the loss of our child.

Lying in a hospital bed, not alone, in this labor ward of screaming women, my child dead in my womb. What did I do wrong? How could God let my child die? Is this my punishment for wrong deeds in the past? I only wanted to be loved and my husband did not love me ... he was still in love with his ex-wife. How did I know? He was never there for me emotionally and in these hours of labor to give birth to our dead daughter, he sat, sat at the foot of my bed, reminiscing to the nurse of memories of his ex-wife. Our baby is dead, the life in her tiny body is gone, her heart stopped, my heart stopped. And he continues, "I caught my ex-wife in bed with another man so I started to drink. I have cirrhosis of the liver." How cruel, I am his wife and our baby will never see the light of day. She is dead.

Meanwhile, the nurse tends to my contractions, monitoring every sign, my blood was clotting, not a good sign. He rambled on to the nurse, did he even notice me lying there? Did he even care? Our baby is dead! My heart was aching, she was not kicking those little precious feet into my stomach, I was not able to save her life.

Lying there, mourning alone. What should I expect from this man who cheated on me from the start of our marriage? Every Friday night I'd park my car in the far lot away from the bowling alley where he bowled. Like a bloodhound I'd wait, then finally he'd walk out the door of the bowling alley with his best friend. Not just the two of them, there were others, two young ladies. I'd follow them to the beach and watch as they left his car and enter a nightclub.

This was his usual routine. Friday nights out with his girlfriend, Saturday with me, and Sunday we went to church. I often wondered if he really thought God would forgive him. I had received many phone calls from friends who had seen him out and about with her and his reply was always the same, "They just want to make trouble for us. There's no truth to what they are saying." I knew different ... the truth, I followed him.

Other women called anonymously to inform me that he was dancing at his favorite honky-tonk bar with his ex-wife. This, too, he denied. Where were his thoughts and emotions as I gave birth to our dead child? He was no use to me, no comfort. The only use was to himself and his memories of her.

Screams from across the room, my eyes targeted a woman in pain, screaming in labor. Our eyes met as she glanced in this still, sterile environment; she, too, was in pain. Pain of a lost child, she was about to give her baby up for adoption. The shame she had brought down on her family, to give birth out of wedlock. These were the 1960s and this was a taboo.

There she lay, alone with no one to comfort her; as she labored, a son was born. My fruitless labor ended ten hours later. The painful memory of legs strapped in stirrups, my body was forced into labor, as abortion was out of the question. My body would not abort on its own. Medication to induce labor was administered and soon the pain was intense. The only memory of this birth was my doctor's words, "Okay, Mary, push."

It was the anesthesiologist's job to knock me out after she was delivered. Then they rolled my bed into a ward on the second floor. This ward was for surgery cases, as my doctor felt I should be away from the cries of babies in the maternity ward. Wrong! As I awoke from the anesthesia, the natural instinct to rest my hands on top of my stomach took place; but the emptiness, no hard body under the flesh and my hands sank into my stomach. My baby was gone, gone forever, no signs of her existence. Where was my fruit? Only emptiness, and my arms aching to hold her, my breast ripe for nursing, no fruit for my labor.

Tears rolled down like pouring rain in a thunder-storm; crying out, I could no longer hold back the bellows and they were heard out into the hallway. Nothing was able to soothe this grief or replace my loss.

***

As a mother of three wonderful sons, I nurtured their every move and fell in the shadows as their bright eyes of innocence dimmed with everyday stresses of adulthood and marriage. Moments in time to remember; rehearsed over and over on the stage of one's mind–it must be perfect. This waltz, he does not need to stand on the toes of your shoes and you no longer need to hold him securely.

Today your son leads you around the dance floor, your heart racing and tears flowing, you gently kiss his cheek and he embraces you in his arms - he towers over you, your child is a man whose new life is about to begin. And your family has a new addition, another child, and a daughter. The bond between mother and son now includes his wife. Or does it?

This dance shared with my son on his wedding day never took place; my dreams were crushed, and the moment I had planned and waited for all those years would not become a memory. Instead, the painful memory of being a guest and not a participant on my son's wedding day leaves scars in my heart. This was her choice. Turning my cheek, wiping my tears, someday she will be the mother of my grandchild and she will bring Bill much joy and I must uncover a piece of my heart to share with her. One day she will long to waltz with her child.

***

True Confessions

Tell a friend, that's what Ms. Zest was always trying to convince me to do. She thought it would help to confide in my children, in a close friend or even my mother. "You need a support system to help you." That's what she would say. Over the past years I did try to tell, and on a few of occasions I succeeded.

I always watched the body language and ... the eyes, the eyes are a dead giveaway. It was hard enough for me to look at them in their faces, but if they couldn't look back at me ... then I would regret my confession. If they ask too many questions and pry, wanting grim details, then I imagined their interest was of gossip – entertaining them at my expense. But when they quickly changed the topic, I would feel humiliated all over again because I knew they were embarrassed. Or, maybe they just didn't want to face the reality that it could have been them who was raped. Did I just taint the image they had of me? Were they feeling vulnerable, too? Do they blame me? Or, do they believe me at all?

I remember the first person I told – this was my Polish friend of many years; our children went to preschool together and our friendship began. In those days we were very close but the children grew up and our lives took a turn – we lost contact for a few years. Dotty, serious in nature, now in her fifties, heard I was divorced so she became a detective searching for a missing person. What a surprise when the phone rang and it was Dotty, after all those years, and within minutes the light had been rekindled and the gap in time had closed.

It was shortly afterward that I confided to her in a phone conversation. In the beginning, when I was recalling events, and as I spoke, my voice would fluctuate, even crack, and as always, the tears flowed. There was no body language or eye movement to be seen through the phone lines but the conversation flowed with no dead airspace and only calmness was in her voice. My ears were tuned up on high alert, listening for any tone in Dotty's voice that cued she was repulsed by the words I spoke. There were clearly no cues, only genuine, loving reinforcement from Dotty's words that it was not my fault ... Then she spoke little and listened a lot. I never really let my guard down completely, but gained comfort in her words.

***

I'm almost eleven years older than my Irish friend Sophia. Her laughter is infectious, it's a constant comedy when she's around. You never know what to expect when she arrives, a redhead, brunette or a blonde. One sure thing you will find .... is a friend. Unlike Dotty, Sophia asks questions and always with the intent to understand and aid in my plight but with the intensity of a Marine Drill Sergeant. I would place road-blocks in her path at times and just like that cross-country runner, hurdle after hurdle, she never lost a beat and in a loving way she would interrogate until she was satisfied. At times I would feel offended by her constant questions and even though Sophia's comment would make me feel on guard, in the end that was her job as a friend.

***

Sometimes when friends would visit I would assess the situation. Is the timing right? Is this the right friend to confide in? Would she disappoint me in her reactions? Well, one day, a very old friend was visiting; we had known each other for nearly thirty-five years and by now she was in her late fifties. You can have old friends that aren't close friends and this was the case. In hindsight I should have put a zip on it.

It was winter of 2002, fireplace burning, lights turned down low and you could smell the fragrance of pine candles burning, we were celebrating my first winter in my new home. She and I had just finished dinner and gone to the living room to relax, listening to soothing piano music.

Thoughts of Ms. Zest and her words of wisdom came rushing into my mind and without thinking I blurted out a brief recap of the rape with anticipation of a positive response from my friend. Lately I've been trying to take advantage of every opportunity to say that word and replay some feelings and each time the scenario reruns, it gets easier. Chills ran down my back as I held my breath waiting for a response........any response. Nothing! Dead air! There was this blank expression on her face, no body movements, she was like a statue. The chill from this stone sculpture filled the air and as my eyes stared across the room in her direction my heart sank in my chest.

How could I have been so very stupid? What now? Moments passed, and revitalizing this dead air took more energy, energy I had to find to wipe out the past few moments and move forward with a new conversation, any conversation. One lesson learned through this – it's to think out the consequences of telling the wrong person. Rejection is painful and at times damaging, you lose faith in your own judgment. Luckily, the chill in the air dissipated as she walked out the door and the light from the stars in the dark winter sky reflecting in the hall mirror warmed my reflection. Maybe this friend has a secret, too.

***

Over these many years I have only shared my story or bits of my story with ten people. There is only one of those ten that I have difficulty with today – that being my son Chris. I would never confide in my mother, as that would be the all time worst case scenario. But two out of three as recommended by Ms. Zest.......well, that's not bad. It didn't kill me. I became stronger and learned a little more of myself in the process. I learned a little more about my friends as well.

It was after the New Year 2004, Chris and I are standing in the kitchen debating on some topic, I am getting upset, not at him but at myself, for something stupid I did. Misdirecting my anger I turned to him and said, "Do you want to know why I'm like this? Huh? Well, I'll tell you!" All the ugliness came out and Chris tried to ask questions. "Who was it, Mom?" He asked. I replied in a very defensive manner and in a loud, stern voice. "It's none of your business!" The timing was all wrong and I hadn't planned to tell Chris, it was a moment of anger that I could not take back. The question from my son, the look on his face, what would he do if I told him who it was? What purpose would it serve? My words were all too harsh, it wasn't his fault – the rape. Just because he wears a baseball cap, just because I thought it could have been him or Paul at the door.

Maybe it was just the cap that was triggering this anger. Chris was innocent, he just wanted to help and wanted to understand, that's all. I just wasn't ready for his help. I wasn't ready to look at my son's eyes and I couldn't look into his eyes. His wonderful, soft, hazel eyes; what would I see in his eyes? Chris left that night with questions unanswered and we've never spoken of the rape again.

I miss our visits, our conversations, the way he used to tease me. My loss is so great I stand sadly alone and feel very much abandoned and unloved. The rape has touched every aspect of my life. Does Chris blame me? Is that why he stays away? Who can guess the motives behind other's actions – mine have always been to protect my children. I pray, someday they will understand.

***

It is January 3, 2004. My mother is aging, confusion and forgetfulness populate her mind everyday and watching this transformation angers me. She has no choice, the aging process is like a run-away train, picking up speed until that sudden impact and she will be gone. This anger within me lashes out at her and at night safe under the blankets I pray to God. "Lord, help me to have patience with my mother and cut this wicked tongue from my mouth. Help me to understand my behavior, open my eyes and guide me." Death is inevitable, it is natural, and we are meant to be with the Lord. I have realized I am not angry with her for showing weakness ... she has no control. Before this sudden impact occurs, my anger must be redirected.

Vicky, my friend of four years, her voice channels through the phone lines almost every day. She has become an opposing mirror for me to pose in front of, remarking on my faults in her distinct accent of broken English. This native-born Yugoslavian utters mere truths and asks, "Is something else bothering you? Maybe you are reacting to your mother this way because of something else. Think about it, Mary. I'm not wanting to hurt your feelings but you have been acting differently. You need to have patience with your mother. Remember she is getting older and if my mother was living here, I would be loving every moment and telling her how much I loved her."

Her frankness was guaranteed. She spoke with the same frankness as when she commented proudly on my weight gain compared to her losses. A mere one hundred and sixteen pounds could not compare to my hefty weight. In both counts she is correct – this opposing mirror reflecting my weakness. I am no longer focused on her spoken words. All cozy, wrapped in my favorite beige-colored fleece blanket, recliner footrest extended out, legs elevated for comfort, then opening up and baring all, hearing myself admit, "I was raped" is less painful and my words spoken, "I am a survivor" actually caused a smile to appear. Vicky's reaction, the gasp for breath was heard through the phone lines and visions of distress formulated her fears as she said, "Oh, my God ... no. You were what?"

She reflects on the first time we met and the months to follow and mentions, "You used to drink a lot back then but I haven't noticed you drinking much anymore." As I described the traumas relived, Vicky identified those behaviors associated with each. Tones in her voice fluctuated, hints of suspicion as she asked, "Mary, what about all those bruises? I always thought there was more going on with you and Paul than you were admitting." She was so serious with suspicion assuming he had battered and abused me.

"Oh, Vicky! No, Paul would never hurt me. I bruised myself at night in my sleep." Somehow I didn't feel more explanations were necessary and Vicky seemed satisfied with this mere synopsis, never asking for more details. Did she truly believe me that I was the abuser of myself? There was a flow of verbs, nouns, adjectives and fragmented sentences and our conversation closed with significance and respect, as it was just a Conversation. Moments of tears, tremors in voice, dissipated in the air. Why? Was it because time was … healing? Had I become desensitized to the word rape? Or, was it the manner in which Vicky embraced my story?

Multiple Traumas

As explained in the book *How Trauma Survivors Learn to Live Again*, by Linda Danials, Psy.D., she is an American Academy board-certified expert in traumatic stress, "Survivors of multiple traumas such as murder of a loved one, or who have survived violence, rape or incest in addition to other violent crimes or have witnessed violence, may have never worked through the previous traumas. In these cases the new trauma triggers emotions tied to these previous traumas and grief takes hold to permeate and becomes a part of their very being. These past traumas must be pulled to the surface and addressed in order to cope with the present one."

***

Well, as life would have it, the above characteristics became obvious as the sessions with Ms. Zest unfolded and the many traumas in my life buried so deep inside began to surface.

Miscarriage:

Newly married, and at a young age of nineteen years, I suffered through a miscarriage and lost my first child, a girl, at eight months into my pregnancy - Dawn Marie would never live to see her siblings.

Intruder:

When I was pregnant with my last child, a young man under the influence of drugs had mistaken our house for his friend's. When the doorbell rang that night I promptly went to answer the door and he forced his way into our home. He grabbed me tight and pushed me into the kitchen almost knocked me to the floor. As I was yelling for my husband and trying to get away, he grabbed me with both hands and was shaking me when my husband came to my rescue. The police were called and the young man was taken away.

The robbery:

I was working at a convenience store in the evenings. My two oldest sons would often walk over at night to help me wash the floors before closing. This evening it was raining and they stayed home. It was a slow evening and there were no customers in the store when I went into the back to stock the cooler with beverages. I could watch for customers through the glass doors of the cooler. One male customer walked into the store and went straight to the counter. I quickly left the cooler and headed straight for the counter to wait on this customer. Once behind the counter, I asked if I could help him. His only reply was to expose his gun to me and with that he said, " Give me your money." I was in shock. As I opened the cash register drawer and handed him the money all I could think was, "Thank goodness my sons aren't here." He kept yelling, "Where is the money, give me all the money." Then all of a sudden a flash of light, a car pulled up in front of the store and a man got out and was walking toward the door. All I could think was that the robber was going to shoot him, shoot me. I was going to be dead and my sons would not have a mother. He had such rage in his eyes, but when he noticed the lights and a person walking toward the door, he fled right through that door, almost knocking over this man. I was traumatized and never returned to this job.

One day I was at the local bank and a gentleman walked in carrying a briefcase. I watched him walk over to the side counter and place the briefcase down and proceed to open it. I just knew he was about to pull out a gun so I ran to the nearest desk and crunched down behind it. There was no gun. When I looked up all these eyes were staring down at me. How foolish I felt. It was a couple of months before I could resume my life as it was before the robbery.

Gene's accident:

My brother was giving his eldest son a party to celebrate his tenth birthday. I was waiting at his house with Jane my eldest son's girlfriend when the call came. It was my sister yelling about her son not having a ride to the party. Off Gene went down the road to pick up our nephew. Shortly after he left the phone rang again, and my sister was crying and yelling "Gene is dead, Gene is dead." I left Jane behind and I raced to my sister's house to find out what was happening. The rescue team was already there and the police had stopped all traffic. As I drove past his car, which was on its side, I could see my brother's legs curled in the windshield, and his head outside the window on the pavement. There were blood drops on his face and his jolly face looked so thin. Later I heard that the underside of Gene's face was gone.

Funeral

Today is December 6, 2004, I am perfectly safe, and to date the demons and nightmares have never darkened my doors.

It was a month back that I wrestled with emotions of whether I should attend a funeral, due to the untimely death of a young man, a relative of a childhood friend. But, if I did this, I would see my attacker. In my mind I envisioned me walking up to the casket then turning to embrace my friend and then staring past her and into his eyes to watch the tears flow from his loss. In my thoughts it was giving me much pleasure to see him in pain, crying from the rape of life that had been taken from him. Did I want to attend this funeral out of respect or for bittersweet revenge?

Turning to the Lord I asked, "Lord, what should I do? My heavenly Father, I offer this up to you, please help me to see what you want of me." My Lord has spoken and I know in my heart forgiveness will set me free. I have forgiven my attacker, my childhood friend - in this year 2004. And with this forgiveness the page turns and a new chapter begins. No, I did not go to the funeral.

Psalm 23

THE LORD IS MY SHEPHERD

The Lord is my shepherd,
I shall not want;
He makes me lie down in green pastures.
He leads me beside still waters;
He restores my soul.
He leads me in paths of righteousness
for His name's sake.

Even though I walk through the valley
of the shadow of death,
I fear no evil;
for You are with me;
Your rod and Your staff, they comfort me.

Surely goodness and mercy shall follow me
all the days of my life;
and I shall dwell in the house of the
Lord forever.

The Package

Today a package arrived in the mail. It was too large to be placed in the mailbox, so the carrier brought it to the door. I signed for it, said, "Thank you," and closed the door. I recognized the handwriting, it was Lillie's. Pray tell, what has she sent me? It's 2005 and we are still making those warm phone calls, writing letters and sending the occasional gifts, what is it this time?

As I pulled back the brown wrapping, I recognized the green box. It's the box I sent to Lillie in 2002, when I was about to move into my new home. It contained the letters and cards Paul had sent over the years. These words at one time had meant so much to me, the words of love, torment and despair.

I had mailed them to her and asked that she keep them until the time came that I wanted them back. Before the move took place, I was clearing out all the excess stuff not needed or wanted and tossing it in the trash. How could I toss out these last attachments to Paul?

So I wrote:

Dear Lillie,

With the upcoming move I am trying to toss out all that stuff that we all collect over the years in hopes that my children will not be burdened with it upon my death. I even found old cards from a boyfriend at the age of fifteen. There is no way I could toss out Paul's letters and ever so often I pull them out, read them, cry a lot, miss him, and put them away again. Every day I still think of him. I go through the motions of moving ahead and my friends say they are proud of my progress, but the reality is, my heart is in pain all the time. After I ran into Paul a few weeks ago when he was on his bike, the thoughts of him have intensified to the point that they interfere with my concentration at work.

Those inevitable flowers came shortly after our paths crossed, but again I was strong and didn't call or respond. One day the following week at about 4:00 AM, Paul left a message on my voice mail at work. He said, he could not get me off his mind, was thinking about me often and could not get past it. He said he was going to write a letter and I should expect it in a day or two. Of course I hung on every word, saved the voice mail and waited. But the letter never came.

I can't call Paul and ask him to leave me alone because with any contact we will just find an excuse to see one another again. If I just don't respond, eventually Paul will lose interest in this game, if that's what it is, and he'll move on.

Lillie, I did go on my trip and even though I thought of Paul, I didn't go searching for the gators he likes. Forgive me for venting; I just have to get it out. I am trusting you with these letters, please don't ever let Paul know you have seen them. I feel a real need to share this part of my life with you. All these written words are the same words Paul still speaks today. Was I crazy to believe in him … in us?

I thought at this age the hunger to have Paul's child would have disappeared, but the past few weeks it too has grown stronger. I don't really know what I expect you to do with these letters other then read them if you choose, please don't toss them out, just keep them safe, as one day I may call to say please return to sender.

Thanksgiving will be here soon, hope it will be one of your best and when you see Paul, just squeeze him a little harder for me. Please excuse my handwriting, I am writing through tears. Please try to understand where I am coming from with all of this. I'm not sure I know!

Your Friend ~ Mary

Walking into the kitchen I was remembering Lillie's last call. "Mary, I have something to tell you. I wanted to make sure you heard it from me first and not someone on the street." "Lillie, what is it?" There was crackling in her voice and a sense of concern. My first thought was that something happened to Paul. She asked me to sit down if I wasn't already ... and she began.

"Paul got married." What did I hear, "No, this can't be." As I listened, she went on. I was in shock of a sort, the tears rolled down my face, I could not hold them back and at one point, I think I even screamed out Paul's name. Deep down I always hoped that one day we would be together again. My world was crashing, no hope of turning back the hands of time. She said something about the ceremony taking place in Maryland, who was there I don't know, as I couldn't focus on her words. The only words I heard were repeated in my mind, "Paul got married ... Paul got married ... Paul got married!"

As I caught my breath, Lillie was saying my name, "Mary, are you okay?" I'm thinking, "No, I'm not okay. I'm healing from the rape, got myself back together and now this. I hung onto Paul's image as I was being raped and then I hung onto his image as I recovered from the rape. What can I hang on to now that he is gone from me forever??"

Trying to hold back the tears and focus on Lillie's words, I could tell she felt my pain. Just before we hung up she said, "They want to start a family right away." I don't remember how we ended our conversation, just that it was a painful one.

As I placed the box on the counter, my thoughts were of the letters in that green box ...... What do I do with this box? I called Lillie to let her know the box had arrived. What do I do with these letters, what do I do?

"Hi, Lillie, it's Mary." I told her the box arrived and I was going to put it in my closet and not read any of the letters. I wasn't ready to toss them out but by the same token, didn't want to open my wounds again. "Did you read the letters?" I asked; she said "No." She didn't feel right to read them as they were private between me and Paul. She just tried to keep them out of sight. Now that Paul was married, she didn't feel comfortable holding them any longer. This was why the package arrived. Of course, I understood. I worried that I would lose my place in her heart now that Paul was married. But Lillie assured me that I would always be dear to her. On that note we said our good-byes.

The Box
by mary

Through smoky skies and blistery winds
This package reached its stop
The postman walks with quickened steps
To leave this glowing box

As snowflakes fall and cardinals fly
To home and her delight
A gift from friend to warm the heart
And cheer the tears within

As time goes on and years pass by
These boxes still arrive
A bond is built and passion flows
With grateful pen she writes

Lord, thank you for these memories
And for this friend so far
And thank you for this life
I live that I may touch the

Stars

Today

Reflecting on this road I've traveled, to finally be at this place in my life, it hasn't been easy and I've fallen along the way, but nonetheless, here I am. The image in the mirror today is pleasing to my eyes, not one of surface beauty, but of courage, strength and wisdom. Things happen for a reason and people come into our lives to teach lessons and if our hearts are open, we will embrace this new-found knowledge and not be afraid to celebrate the future as life unfolds.

From the closet of time, I pull out that new virgin canvas and begin to paint with wild fury, utilizing all the vibrant colors from heaven. My brush is no longer restricted to those shades of *green*, my attacker and childhood friend Tony, *red* the victim myself and *yellow* for my love Paul. The boundaries of that triangle are lifted and I have been freed. Like the maintenance crew driving on the golf course in their trailers, picking up dead branches that have fallen during the destructive winds of the winter and raking up all the decayed leaves, my winter maintenance has been done, too.

All the dead and decayed gathered up and burned in a fire of depression, post-traumatic stress, alcohol addiction, self-medicating, over-eating and self-mutilation. Released in this smoke of fire were all the tainted images, nightmares and demons.

Last week I walked along the beach at Misquamicut, slightly guarded but not afraid. I exchanged greetings with others and smiled at the men. Looking out at the horizon on this last week in February 2005, the day was almost as clear as last September and yes, the bluffs on Block Island appeared to be in sight.

The waves tumbled toward shore one after another, three rows deep – endless foam rushed to my feet and with damp sneakers I stepped back and planted my backside onto the sand, then glanced up into the cloud-filled heavens and gave thanks to the Lord for this day. My thoughts were of how far I've come from the baseball season of 1996 and the rape. If it weren't for the turmoil of work and medical problems, the memories of the rape might have taken much longer to resurface and it was four years before a trigger opened Pandora's box in the year 2000. The smell of the salt air reminded me of all the tears that had rolled down my cheeks and landed near my lips ... that salty taste of recovery, which has taken five years.

As dogs on leashes run down the beach, grains of sand flip up into the air and their masters trot behind. Where were they in 1996? Would the year 2005 be significant for them? The temperature begins to drop and the figures walking the beach appear to fade as distance lengthens between us and my exhaled breath can be seen in the crisp air. I too, must leave for home. Brushing the damp sand from my backside, I begin my journey down the beach but after traveling but a few feet, the sound of a seagull gains my attention and I turn. As the seagull takes flight, sand drops from his feet and my eyes follow this sight to the ground. What I saw was one set of footprints and I am reminded that I was never alone in my journey of life.

The Lord was always with me.
Guiding, comforting and giving me strength.
2005 will be a Wonderful Year!

Soon the colors of spring will fill the landscapes and my golf clubs will be polished, ready for play. It will be a time of new births and budding flowers, the scent of air-dried laundry and warm spring showers, everything pure and wonderful.

I Have Closure

It must come full circle to have closure and this is the day, July 19, 2005 ... closure is mine. I had just asked the Lord, why?

I was enjoying the company of my sister and her husband, sitting at the bar of a local restaurant when "WHO" walks in? He just sat there, at the bar, opposite me, and I glanced up. The air in my lungs froze and my heart sank. It's been three plus years and he's not changed ... if only he sat closer, his scent – oh, that sweet scent.

As he acknowledged my presence with a gentle smile and idle conversation – "How's your mom? Heard you have a beagle." I could feel my throat start to tighten. My eyes were focused on his eyes, and from the distance between us, I could not tell if his soul was open. The sounds of laughter surrounding me had muffled and the only other words invading my ears were the words of my sister asking her husband, "Who is she talking to?" Then she turned and looked down at her leg that was being squeezed with much pressure. This automatic response was my way of letting her know without words that I was emotional.

And yes, Paul continued to hold my attention, feeding information as to his relocation to Maryland and now living in his grandparents' farmhouse. As he continued, my thoughts drifted and the emotions and visions of the past month filled my mind. The energy forces that surged through my body during that time all made sense to me now.

Lillie will be fifty-years-old on July 25th and I had been preparing a Power Point presentation on CD, with pictures and stories as one of her gifts to celebrate her life. Paul had often spoken of the farm and the last I knew a family of color was renting it. But, the energy I felt over this past month as visions of the farmhouse came to the foreground were vacant of color and warm with comfort and belonging. At the time it seemed trivial and not worth analyzing. Now it all made sense, that energy force was his.

I was reminded of another time that energy had alerted me. Paul had gone to Louisiana, his grandmother was in the hospital and the situation was grim, she was not expected to last but a few days. In the early morning, as my restless body tossed and turned, I tried to open my eyes but this very bright light from nowhere was shining into them.

Each time I tried to open my eyes the light was so bright that the lids retreated and closed tight as to protect my eyes. My first thought was that someone was there shining a flashlight into them. But, I was alone. A short while later Paul called to give me the news ... Grandma had passed away. I already knew!

As Paul slowly sipped on his beer, I began planning my escape, not to be sitting here and watching his back as he walked away. And, I could not be sitting here alone with him as my sister left for home. The tighter my throat became, emotions were about to erupt and the tears were soon to come. Yes, he still owned that place in my heart. I wished we could talk about that night but what was the point?

Quickly opening my purse and getting out the car keys, I leaned into my sister's face and kissed her cheek, "I'm leaving," I told her and when she asked "Why," my reply was, "I have work to do at home." Before these tears erupt, I turned to Paul and said, "Bye, Paul, it was so good to see you again." The escape mode had set in and there is no recollection of his words. By the time I had reached the door, there was no holding back the tears and as I walked to my car there was this sense of comfort.

Paul no longer stands in the shadow of my attacker. His memory can now stand alone. The Lord had just answered my original question, "Why?" And as always I gave the Lord thanks for allowing this closure.

Writing This Book

In writing this book I've gained a great deal of knowledge in the area of rape survival, through the reading of many stories written by survivors, as well as researching statistics and articles on rape. In the infancy of my writings I felt isolated in the traumatic experiences which followed the rape to the degree that I felt I was a freak and my emotions were those of a crazy woman. Not true, the many facets that compose trauma are real and to some degree are experienced by all victims of rape.

All the therapeutic steps taken over the past years to recover from this trauma, the private counseling sessions, art therapy, talking to friends, counseling through the Rape Crisis Center were positive experiences. In the end the writing of this book was the tool which helped me to solidify my recovery. I spent many hours in front of my computer just recalling moments in time, reliving the pain and crying. These tears were tears of joy that the road traveled had come to an end and I had found forgiveness in my heart.

Throughout my life I've tried to turn negative experiences into positive ones and this was no different. I feel the Lord is using me as a tool to help others, to share my story and the triumph, the victory, which is mine.

As I walk the streets today, calm and confident – fear does creep in, and in the darkest moment shadows fall and the memories reach out like a baby's arm extended high into the air with anticipation of the stability and comfort its creator (mother) will provide. I, too, reach out through the fog of torment and embrace these fears, which empower me to move on. Honeysuckle is sweet and can intoxicate one's senses, breathe deep, breathe deep, remember this sweet scent.

Epilogue

Remember, I mentioned it must come full circle to have closure, and in 2005 I thought it had as Paul no longer stood in the shadow of my attacker. It's now 2016 and on a trip to Staples to make copies of documents, I experienced a flashback. No, not in my mind, but one I had worried about for many years. What would I do if Tony appeared out of nowhere? Today was that day – March 17th.

All dressed in black accented with a green feathered wrap, you know the drill, must wear a hint of green to celebrate St. Paddy's Day. There I was, walking to my car on this bright sunny day thinking about the fun I was about to enjoy with friends, when a voice from nowhere was yelling out my name. At first I didn't recognize him, this aged figure with gray hair. Suddenly my happy thoughts were erased and fear took its place.

Quickly I stepped into my car and he kept coming and yelling "Mary, don't you know who I am?" I just wanted a quick getaway so I said, "No." He replied with, "I'm Tony. Don't you remember me? I see you on TV, you have a show on Public Access. How are you doing? You look scared." Every limb in my body was shaking and tears were about to flow. All I could think was; "Get away! Get away!" Then I yelled back, "Our last confrontation was not a good one." He stood there, just looking at me as I pulled out of the parking spot. He hung his head and the smile left his face as he walked away.

As I drove to the post office to purchase stamps the words, "You look scared" kept running through my mind. I wanted to yell out, "You raped me, you raped me. How can you not remember what you did to me?" It was hard to focus as I walked up to the counter to purchase stamps, holding back my emotions. As I turned to leave, Christine's husband was there, calling out to get my attention – attention I was happy to give him, as he knew my story. When I shared what had taken place just fifteen minutes earlier, he smiled and said, "You know we are here for you." I reached out my arms to hug him and he held me tight ... I felt comfort.

It's just a short drive to my house and once there I sat in the driveway thinking. Why now? As emotional as I felt, there was this empowerment. Was this in the Lord's plans? I did confront Tony with my statement,"Our last confrontation was not a good one." It was not a confrontation -- it was an attack. I put it on him, as Lillie said. Yes, it was Lillie I called to share my feelings of this event. Her words, "He was drunk. He has to live with it." I had forgiven him in 2004, but had never seen him after the rape, until now. The sight of Tony frightened me, but the demons and visions of that night have never reappeared, and I do feel empowered by our chance meeting. He will never again rob me of my peace of mind; I have come full circle and I am free!

The Effects of Acquaintance Rape

Perspectives on Acquaintance Rape
David G. Curtis, Ph.D., B.C.E.T.S.
Clinical Associate, Long Island Psychological Associates, P.C.
http://www.aaets.org/arts/art13.htm

The consequences of acquaintance rape are often far-reaching. Once the actual rape has occurred and has been identified as rape by the survivor, she is faced with the decision of whether to disclose to anyone what has happened. In a study of acquaintance rape survivors (Wiehe & Richards, 1995), 97 percent informed at least one close confidant. The percentage of women who informed the police was drastically lower, at 28 percent. A still smaller number (twenty percent) decided to prosecute. Koss (1988) reports that only two percent of acquaintance rape survivors report their experiences to the police. This compared with the 21 percent who reported rape by a stranger to the police. The percentage of survivors reporting the rape is so low for several reasons. Self-blame is a recurring response, which prevents disclosure. Even if the act has been perceived as rape by the survivor, there is often an accompanying guilt about not seeing the sexual assault coming before it was too late. This is often directly or indirectly reinforced by the reactions of family or friends in the form of questioning the survivor's decisions to drink during a date or to invite the assailant back to their apartment, provocative behavior, or previous sexual relations. People normally relied upon for support by the survivor are not immune to subtly blaming the victim. Another factor which inhibits reporting is the anticipated response of the authorities. Fear that the victim will again be blamed adds to apprehension about interrogation. The duress of re-experiencing the attack and testifying at a trial, and a low conviction rate for acquaintance rapists, are considerations as well.

The percentage of survivors who seek medical assistance after an attack is comparable to the percentage reporting to police (Wiehe & Richards, 1995). Serious physical consequences often emerge and are usually attended to before the emotional consequences. Seeking medical help can also be a traumatic experience, as many survivors feel like they are being violated all over again during the examination. More often than not, attentive and supportive medical staff can make a difference. Survivors may report being more at ease with a female physician. The presence of a rape-crisis counselor during the examination and the long periods of waiting that are often involved with it can be tremendously helpful. Internal and external injury, pregnancy, and abortion are some of the more common physical after effects of acquaintance rape.

Research has indicated that the survivors of acquaintance rape report similar levels of depression, anxiety, complications in subsequent relationships, and difficulty attaining pre-rape levels of sexual satisfaction to what survivors of stranger rape report (Koss & Dinero, 1988). What may make coping more difficult for victims of acquaintance rape is a failure of others to recognize that the emotional impact is just as serious. The degree to which individuals experience these and other emotional consequences varies based on factors such as the amount of emotional support available, prior experiences, and personal coping style. The way that a survivor's emotional harm may translate into overt behavior also depends on individual factors. Some may become very withdrawn and uncommunicative, others may act out sexually and become promiscuous. Those survivors who tend to deal the most effectively with their experiences take an active role in acknowledging the rape, disclosing the incident to appropriate others, finding the right help, and educating themselves about acquaintance rape and prevention strategies.

One of the most serious psychological disorders which can develop as the result of acquaintance rape is Post-traumatic Stress Disorder (PTSD). Rape is just one of many possible causes of PTSD, but it (along with other forms of sexual assault) is the most common cause of PTSD in American women (McFarlane & De Girolamo, in van der Kolk, McFarlane, & Weisaeth, 1996). PTSD as it relates to acquaintance rape is defined as in the Diagnostic and Statistical Manual of Mental Disorders-Fourth Edition as "the development of characteristic symptoms following exposure to an extreme traumatic stressor involving direct personal experience of an event that involves actual or threatened death or serious injury, or other threat to one's physical integrity" (DSM-IV, American Psychiatric Association, 1994). A person's immediate response to the event includes intense fear and helplessness. Symptoms which are part of the criteria for PTSD include persistent re-experiencing of the event, persistent avoidance of stimuli associated with the event, and persistent symptoms of increased arousal. This pattern of re-experiencing, avoidance, and arousal must be present for at least one month. There must also be an accompanying impairment in social, occupational, or other important realm of functioning (DSM-IV, APA, 1994).

If one takes note of the causes and symptoms of PTSD and compares them to thoughts and emotions which might be evoked by acquaintance rape, it is not difficult to see a direct connection. Intense fear and helplessness are likely to be the core reactions to any sexual assault. Perhaps no other consequence is more devastating and cruel than the fear, mistrust, and doubt triggered by the simple encounters and communication with men which are a part of everyday living. Prior to the assault, the rapist had been indistinguishable from non rapists. After the rape, all men may be seen as potential rapists. For many victims, hyper-vigilance towards most men becomes permanent. For others, a long and difficult recovery process must be endured before a sense of normalcy returns.

RESOURCES

The following reading materials and websites can be quite helpful to you, the survivor of rape, in managing your recovery. Friends and relatives of loved ones who have suffered this traumatic experience will gain insights to that nightmare and a better understanding of life after rape.

After Silence Rape & My Journey Back
by Nancy Venable Raine
Copyright 1998
Crown Publishers, Inc.
201 East 50th Street
New York, New York 10022

This is a story of her recovery from rape and those who helped her along the way. If you are interested in statistics, quotes from journals, magazines and reference materials you will find this book of value.

Free of the Shadows
Recovering from Sexual Violence
by Caren Adams, M.A. & Jennifer Fay, M.A.
Copyright 1989
New Harbinger Publications, Inc.
5674 Shattuck Ave.
Oakland, CA 94608

This book was written as case studies of a few rape victims' story. There is a section for guidance for the families of that victim and a section for guidance to the victim on how to cope with their questions of the events. The back sections of this book are notes for Therapists and a resource section with a list of reading materials.

Telling
A Memoir of Rape and Recovery
by Patricia Weaver Francisco
Copyright 1999
Harper Collins Publishers, Inc.
10 East 53rd Street
New York, New York, 10022

This is the author's story of her rape and the ten-year recovery period. During those years she had met other rape survivors and at one point the story takes you the reader through her insights as she sat through a rape trial and watched the outcome unfold.

The Rape Recovery Handbook
Step-by-Step Help for Survivors of Sexual Assault
by Aphrodite Matsakis, PH.D.

This book copyright 2003

New Harbinger Publications, inc.

5674 Shattuck Avenue

Oakland, CA 94609

Website – www.matsakis.com

In this book you will learn how to manage the emotional pain caused by the trauma of a sexual assault and coping with the reality of this experience. Dealing with conflicting and debilitating feelings with the aftermath of the assault.

RAINN
Rape Abuse & Incest National Network

Website – www.rainn.org

The Rape, Abuse & Incest National Network (RAINN) is the nation's largest anti-sexual assault organization. RAINN operates the National Sexual Assault Hotline at 1.800.656.HOPE and carries out programs to prevent sexual assault, help victims and ensure that rapists are brought to justice. Inside, you'll find statistics, counseling resources, prevention tips, news and more.

This website is a great resource to locate the nearest Rape Crisis Center in your area; all you need to do is click on Counseling Centers and insert your zip code.

WASH IT AWAY

Made in the USA
Middletown, DE
14 May 2016